Promises

New Edition

BETTY LOWREY

ISBN 979-8-9906818-7-3 (paperback)
ISBN 979-8-9906818-6-6 (eBook)

Scriptures marked KJV are taken from the KING JAMES VERSION (KJV): KING JAMES VERSION, public domain.

Printed in the United States of America

Contents

For Bob and those who follow in his footsteps

Acknowledgement

My sincere appreciation to:
Colonel (Ret.) Brian S. Norman USAF

Prologue

Ecclesiastes 3 To everything there is a season, and a time to every purpose under the heaven; There are some things hurt so much, all you can do is think about them but you can't talk about them. Then one day you want to tell someone.

"Don't you see, Julie," Mark whispered. His voice was hoarse. The pleading in his eyes deepened with pain. "It's eating your heart out and mine too. We have to talk about it."

She stared at him, the shrunken body that had once been so strong and the watery eyes once sparkling blue that now the doctors said were going blind and the pain, wrinkling his body, his mind, pushing him up into a form less than human while the core of life struggled on. Where had time gone? It seemed only yesterday they had climbed the branches of the old tree. Now they were adults, but then they were children.

Life had not dealt a fair hand. Willing to serve his country, Mark returned unable to find employment. There were no welcome home signs or bands playing. It seemed Vietnam soldiers were to be pitied but not embraced. "There are promises, Mark," his grandmother had said, "Never forget and always believe."

PROMISES

Betty Lowrey

Mark sat under the old mulberry tree hidden from his sister's view by the spreading branches of the snowball bush with its round clumps of white flowers. Momma had pushed him out the door as soon as he'd eaten, saying, "Go on now, mind yourself and be good. I've much to do." He could hear her putting away the breakfast dishes as he settled down on the damp ground, digging with chubby fingers around the roots of the bush to examine the tiny black bugs and a couple of fat white worms. It was his intention to stay out of Julie's sight, not wishing to help her with her chores.

He maneuvered carefully around the rose bushes. Somehow roses and Momma went together. Just as he'd known, the radio clicked on, bringing her favorite gospel program through the open screened window. The minister's voice twangy and wavering cried out. "They shall mount up with wings of eagles. They shall run and not be weary; and they shall walk and not faint. Isaiah gives us many promises, ours to receive."

Engrossed in the promises, Mark heard no more of the preacher's words. "When I get big," he thought, "I'm going to talk about Jesus. I'll sweat and scream and walk the aisles waving my arms, saving souls. I'll tell them about hell-fire and damnation." Rolling the last words in his mind, Mark's heart fluttered and heaved beneath the thin home-made shirt. "Just think, wings like eagles; run and not be weary. No one will faint. No crippled feet hanging over shoes like Aunt Ora's. No crippled back that's drawn up in a hump, like Uncle Charlie's. Heal the sick. Heal the sinner if they wait upon the Lord."

Looking up to Heaven, Mark whispered, "And Momma won't be tired." In his mind, all Sarah Buchannan did was work. "Momma," he whispered again. "My Momma, Sarah Buchannan."

"There you are." Julie pounced on him. "You come help me water Mother's petunias. You can carry a bucket as good as me."

Mark used one of his father's curse words. Sliding to one side, he pulled a thorn from his finger. "You made me stick that thing clear through my finger, Julie."

"You better shut up that cussin'. Daddy'll beat your butt." Julie giggled. "I heard you. I bet you was preachin,' too. The two don't go together. You can't cuss if you're gonna preach. Now come on."

Every year they watered the roses for Momma and then the petunias. When you're young and can't tell the seasons, sometimes it seems the watering of plants goes on forever.

"Tell me a story, Julie. It makes the time go faster." Mark's eyes lit up. "One that will make us forget we have to get water out of that old ditch."

"There's nothing going to hurt you, Mark." Julie was cautiously examining the ground around the honeysuckle vine that trailed down to the water's edge and the old lilac bush next to it, while her brother waited patiently.

"Daddy said there's been twenty one cottonmouths killed right here," Mark whispered. "Is that what you're looking for? Do they live in those bushes?"

Julie shrugged her shoulders. "I don't think so. Personally, I think that's where the fairies live; in all that good smelling fragrance. Just breathe deep, Mark. Don't you smell it?"

Mark breathed deep, silent, thinking. "I'm not sure there are fairies, Julie. Grandma says all good things come from God and this bush smells good."

Sensing a small portion of her authority had slipped away Julie stared at her brother. Disdaining, she laughed, a ridiculous scornful laugh. "Who's she to know? All she does is boss me and Momma around but you are her golden boy."

"Grandma reads the bible," Mark replied in his soft reasoning voice that dismissed any accusations and left Grandma completely holy and right. "She reads the Bible to me."

Water sloshed from the buckets as they walked; to dry white and flaky on their skin in the hot sun. "I wish she'd read fairy tales to me. She doesn't like me." Julie said matter of fact. "She just likes you."

"Oh, Julie, you can read. I'm not Grandma's what kind of boy was that?"

"Golden boy." Julie's chin jutted obstinately forward. Her mind was made up and she'd heard that expression on the radio and once Daddy's friend, Red said, *"Jorney, you must be old man Fritz golden boy? You got no money and no corn but he gives you credit when he won't the rest of us."* She remembered that conversation. "It means you are special to someone," she explained. "Golden, does."

"You tell the best stories, Julie. You make me feel warm inside like when Momma pulls the covers up and sits on my bed every night. You are the best, Julie."

Resigned, accepting his admiration, she relaxed. After all, what could you do against an old lady with white hair? Suddenly she felt guilty, thinking of all the times Grandma fried apricot pies for her and fried potatoes, too. Momma and Grandma's conversation sang in her mind.

Once, Sarah questioned, "Isn't that a little too much fried food?"

"On a regular basis, I suppose," Grandma replied, "But she'll live over it. We have our special times when she comes to visit." Meaning, Mark received his special foods, too, when he was with Grandma. Julie remembered the day Mark was born. Grandma arrived, brisk as usual, busy and bossy. "Shew, go on now, out of the way. This is no place for you." Momma was laying there on that squeaky bed, hurting with pain written all over her face.

"How you gonna get that baby out of Momma's stomach?" She'd hung on to the bed post, stubbornly questioning, standing her ground against grandma's authority, finally to follow her to the kitchen.

"God provides." Grandma was busy boiling water in a pan on the stove. Going out, returning with clean white sheets, examining them, choosing one to tear long strips, ignoring Julie's stares. "Get now," she said and someone took Julie's hand and led her from the kitchen.

When they allowed her back in, she tiptoed across the cold linoleum floor with its blue background and bright red cabbage roses. Momma lay in the middle of the bed, a small gray knot with wisp of dampness around her hair line, gray eyes watching Julie approach and there in a funny basket like bed lay the new baby.

He wasn't much to look at. Impressive, perhaps he was, in tiny perfection but a bit red with little fingers and dents and wrinkles here and there. What could she say? He was just a baby. Then he opened his eyes, smoky blue, almost black staring into a world full of air and light. The little mouth yawned, making a sucking sound. The little arms waved fitful in the air. Someone leaned to cover him. Now she saw only the little round head but the stormy blue eyes were still watching her. Blink. Blink. He didn't look angry or anything; just looking her over. And she knew right then she loved him.

"Na-na-na-na-na-na." Julie turned abruptly. She didn't like that voice. Daddy's friend sang, "Julie's not the baby. Julie's not the baby." Daddy's friend, red faced and smirking stood in the doorway singing his teasing song. She didn't like him. Julie looked at Momma and then back to Red. Momma pulled herself into a sitting position, an expression of hurt and pain covering her face as Julie ran from the room.

She hid in the kitchen behind the cook stove by the flu that carried the wood smoke up through the wall and out into the air. Sometimes she stood in the yard watching a curl of smoke come out of the chimney, a fog on the roof top. Right now she didn't care where the smoke curled from. She was thankful Grandma wasn't in the room preparing a meal. She would be soon, the stove was warm and the water rumbled in the reservoir as it heated.

Feeling comfortable and sure no one was watching, her attention was drawn to a black spider crawling over and in between sticks of wood. She could kill it in one grinding mash of her shoe but there was the chance it might bite her and she might die. It would serve them all if she died, especially Daddy's friend, Red. It would be his fault.

She listened, from her hiding place. Voices came from the front of the house. The back of the stove wasn't as interesting as the front. She crawled around to the front to trace her fingers around the alphabet letters spaced across the oven door on that cream colored wonder. Then the back door squeaked and Julie scurried to hide in the dark corner again. There was the shuffle of feet, the thump of rubber boots on the floor and her daddy's friend's voice, muffled, while the feet came closer, four soiled socked feet in her view, now between the curved legs of the stove.

"So you've had a hard day, eh?"

"Yeah, started off kind of scary, grew worse as the day wore on."

"How's that?"

The two pulled heavy wooden chairs from the table; Momma's only good strong piece of furniture sent from her mother somewhere across the field because Grandmamma said she was moving to a smaller house and wouldn't need it. The round oaken table replaced a wobble-legged make- shift with chairs so light they tipped over when a person was rising.

"You want coffee, Red?"

"Don't mind if I do, but what's been troubling about this day, Jorney? You got your boy. Isn't that what every man wants, a son to carry on his name?"

Julie scrunched forward, tight legged and quiet, listening; hearing Daddy yawn as he sit opposite Red.

"Didn't get much sleep last night. Sarah started having pain right after we went to bed. No signs 'til this morning, though. The mattress was wet, a bit of other, you know." He yawned again. "I was going out to feed the mules and then go get Ma to help with the birthing."

"Your Ma's probably helped out with every baby around here. She knows what she's doin'."

Julie heard the greedy slurp Red made as he drank coffee.

"Yes, sir. Missus Buchanan knows and ought to, havin' six of her own. Always heard six was a bad number, guess it was alright for your ma, though." Red stumbled to his feet. "I'll take a bit more coffee, Jorney, while you tell me what you'd started on the way in, about them horses."

"Well we went to feed that mule. Dang beast hemmed me into the corner of the barn and kicked at me. Slamming hoofs, I tell you he had fire in his eyes and I was pressed tight against the wall dodging him whatever best way I could. I tell you, it was inch by inch toward the door. I thought he was going to kill me."

"Was it old Jude, the mean one?"

"It was. Had me pressed tight, I tell you, against the wall."

"Bad sign, Jorney." Red's voice sounded mystical, all knowing to Julie. "Bad sign, Jorney."

"That's just half of it. Finally got down to Ma's. Come back, Sarah in pain, I said I'm going for the doctor and Ma's feelings got ruffled. She said she could handle the job."

"And she could."

"I was scared, Red, real bad. I couldn't take chance. Sarah's none too big with the baby. You don't want to lose your wife."

"Don't know 'bout that," Red replied. "Havin' none myself. Got no need for just one woman. Plenty boozers in town, waitin' for you when you want one. Little money. Little whiskey, they're yours."

Julie didn't like that. Momma wasn't a boozer.

"Sarah's a good woman, Red. I hated to see her suffer."

"You're right. She's different. You're a lucky man, Jorney."

Julie relaxed a little, but she hadn't known Grandma couldn't handle Momma's birthin.'

"Dr. Reynolds came back with me. It was a dry birth, which made it hard on Sarah, the baby too."

"Bad sign." Red's sublime voice intoned, "Born in trouble, die in trouble."

"Lord, man, where do you get all your sayins?"

"Well, patch, Jorney, everybody knows I concoct a few. A man don't need too many. But there's enough old wives tales to last a life time." Red guffawed. "Ain't you got no whiskey to celebrate, Jorney?"

Julie was hung up on Red's words. Momma forbade him to curse in her house, so Red said *patch*.

Daddy moved to the old cupboard in the corner, stooping low to pull a flask from behind the tall platter at the back. Julie heard the clink of glass against glass, again and again.

"Jorney, you remember Anna and them old mules?"

"Don't remind me. A release of tension in the tone, the whiskey numbing his brain, John Buchannan's body relaxed as his words continued. "Don't even say it out loud."

"Anna was full of trouble, that night......wheee."

Tears streamed silently down Julie's face, disappointment sore around her heart. So Daddy knew another woman, once, just like Red; a boozer that kept him away from his wife.

"Anna," Red sniggered, slapping his thigh. "Sixteen mules on the run. Wild. I never seen nothin' like it. You chasin' ever which direction. How'd we ever get them mules home?" His ludicrous laughter rolled through the room. "Anna, Illinois."

Click. Bottle to glass. "What's the most mules you ever worked at one time, Jorney?"

"About thirty two head," was Daddy's reply. "Thirty two head of untrained mules, at various stages, of course. But thirty two head on new ground stumps? Green hand drivers and barely enough money to buy corn."

"And you thought this morning was bad?" Red's voice boomed.

John Buchannan stared across the room. "Buy two and three year olds, break, work them and sell them for maybe a hundred dollar profit." He sighed heavily. "Lord, what a man won't do to feed his family."

From her secret post, Julie watched them. Red's face grew redder, the veins standing out on his bulbous nose while both men convulsed in occasional laughter. Daddy's wide shoulders would shake and then his face would line with a sort of sadness over something he knew but wasn't saying. Somehow Julie knew, without question, someday there'd be something to make her face sad and her laughter ring hollow. It was like a heartbeat that beat down through the years, taken for granted and then one day something happens.

The next days were not so awful. The aunts came to see the baby bringing with them their own children who were instructed to play quietly, or, *"I'll take you home."* Viola came in April when the sunlight had warmed the ground and Julie was allowed to go barefoot and Viola brought Daniel.

With their shoes off Julie and Daniel wandered the yard, examining thick clumps of water grass behind Daddy's tool shed and watched the cattle grazing in the pasture. One stout short legged bull caught Daniel's attention.

"He's a mean one, all right." Daniel said. "You can tell by the way he stands glaring at you." He cast his knowledgeable head toward the sky, one eye squinting, "Of course, you know, many a man's been gored by a bull."

Julie crept closer to Daniel's side. "You mean that's why my daddy said never go in the barn lot?"

"Yep, reckon that's so."

She was always amazed that Daniel knew so much, him being six days younger than her.

"Billy's got a cart now for his goat." Billy was Daniel's older brother.

"Can we ride in it?"

"Shucks, no, he won't let us." Daniel dug his hands deep into the pockets of his worn brown trousers. "Don't want to anyway. Dang goat's too wild. Runs all over the place and first time they hooked him to the cart he ran up the old loading shoot."

Julie stared at Daniel.

"You know. Where they drive the cattle through when they're taking them to market. It's high on one end so's it's level with the truck bed. Heh." Daniel was laughing. "Old Billy's goat cart turned upside down, the goat broke loose but it sure thumped old Billy's head. Whee." Daniel turned a somersault on the ground. "Wait 'til old Billy's gone one day. We'll hook that cart up to that goat and we'll take a ride."

"Where's he going?" Billy wasn't old enough to go far.

"Who knows? Who cares?" Daniel turned a double somersault. "He's always sneakin' off, thumbin' rides. Daddy's gonna beat, *you know* out of him if he don't stop."

Indignant, Julie said, "You're daddy don't talk bad."

"Yeah? But your daddy's friend, Red does. He's tough." Daniel climbed up in a tree. "Hey, you still sit on your Momma's lap? I bet that new baby took your place, didn't he?"

A curious thought appeared to Julie "Do you still sit on your Momma's lap?"

"Shucks no," Daniel lied. Daniel thought he was cursing, like Red, when he used big words. He wanted to. He'd tried using a few to make his stories more colorful but Viola heard and whipped his pants.

Julie could just see him sitting there, on Viola's lap, feet dangling to the floor and he thought he knew so much. He wasn't so smart after all.

Daniel strut across the yard, wearing an expression of nonchalance on his face. "You gonna stand there all day?"

Chapter Two

A time to plant and a time to pluck up

Momma planted the garden in April on an unreasonably warm day for that time of the year. Rows and rows of vegetable seed which would in time fill shelves of mason fruit jars, lined by color and name in the pantry. The potatoes planted soon after Mark's birth were green on the ground. Julie examined the plants, aware Grandma was there as usual telling Momma about the signs in the almanac, as she watched Mark in his wicker basket. She'd tried giving advice to Daddy but he wasn't taking it and sent her in from the field. He followed a short time later.

"I'm not abiding it, Ma, your being in the field trying to relegate authority to my men. It's a man's job we're doing and we'll do it."

"Hmph." Grandma blustered, fumed and stepped around the yard with her feet making short crisp steps. "I was farming when you were nothing but a boy wresting your brothers." Baby Mark bounced on her shoulder, doubtlessly thinking it was all for his benefit.

"I'll have no woman making a fool out of me," John Buchanan replied. "Least of all my own mother. You should think better of yourself. Do you wish to be the laughing stock of this community?"

"What do I care what they think of me? It's a bit late for that with me having raised six boys and toiling behind the rump of a mule all day." She glared back as strongly at her son as he did her. "You remember that, don't you? I fed and clothed you, didn't I?" There'd been a moment of silence. "Hmph," she'd finally said, laying Mark in his basket and taking a hoe to dig furiously a trench into which Sarah had strewn beans.

It was the cotton choppers that held Julie and Mark's interest. Late May, they came and the leader's song poured forth each morning, the melody carrying for miles to the accompaniment of swinging hoes and swishing pant legs as the group filed from end to end on the long rows and progressed across the fields, cutting away weeds from cotton plants as the negro spirituals went on. Mark's eyes would light up and stare at the world while a smile played on his face.

"I declare that baby likes singing," Grandma would say.

Julie walked the yard behind the grove of oak trees listening to the deep rhythm of the leader. His song spoke of troubled times even when the words were chorused by the others and she knew it was not of their time but perhaps belonged to those who came before them.

Early in the morning, sometimes before she was out of bed the mournful songs pressed through the air. *Nobody knows...the trouble...I've seen... nobody know...but Jesus....*Heavy, emotional and melancholy the rich voices wailed and carried for miles until by mid-morning *Swing low, Sweet Chariot,* broke into being.

"Daddy, who's that man singing?" She watched as her father fixed a harness inside the old shed.

"It's Joe, little girl."

"Why does he save Swing Low until last?"

"Because his people are getting tired from all the walking. Do you hear the others join in?" He rose up to listen to the words of song wafting across the field. "They had kind of quit for a while, now they forget they're tired and sing because they have something to think about." For a moment, John sang, "*coming for to carry me* home. *I looked over Jordan and what did I see, comin' for to carry me home?*"

She liked when he sang. His eyes softened, as he stared across the field, his hands hung loose and then he was all brisk again returning to work. Julie crept back, weaving through the shadow of the trees to see Mark was inside the porch listening to the plaintive dejection start up again. Sorrowful, they were humming now. *Hmmmmm. Hmmmm.* She wondered what it was they mourned for.

From the window Julie watched a big truck with a long bed pull in the driveway. Her father came out of the small shop. Leaning into the other side of the truck where the driver had opened the window, they were talking about something but Julie couldn't hear. She was edging toward the door when Momma said, "Where you going, honey?"

"Out there to see what Daddy's doing."

"Not now. Wait until they unload the wood, then you can go. You might get run over."

"What's the wood for?"

"Everyone went in together, a few dollars so it wouldn't cost one person too much." Sarah joined Julie, momentarily, looking out the window. "All the musicians got together and decided on Saturday nights they would meet to play music and with nothing else to do they know folks will come to listen."

"But what's the wood for, Momma?" Daddy and the man were stacking it by the shed.

"They need a platform to sit up higher, so the people can see them."

"What will the people sit on, Momma?"

Sarah returned to the stove to stir the beans and check on the corn bread in the oven. "That's a good question. I don't know. Maybe they'll bring a chair or a quilt for on the ground. I just don't know."

Thus began a Saturday night gathering when the work week ended. The people arrived to sit around the plank platform with conversation flowing as they settled down to listen to the music, but when crops needed tending they were fewer in number. It was a different music; unlike the cotton choppers handed down spirituals, the fiddles and guitars brought waltz and ballads and a new kind of music John Buchanan would laugh and explain to Julie, "Why it's for a jig, little girl," and he would grab Sarah by the hand and swing her around, but it was the waltz Julie liked most. When Daddy took Momma in his arms and they danced around the room with him humming and smiling, his eyes were bright with love.

Music claimed John Buchanan like nothing else, it was the whisper of the future; forgotten moments from the past and he lost the irritableness that had become a dark thread of poison spewing forth when he or his family least expected it. Those times he escaped; away from the family to work off the excess energies at some strenuous job until the storm inside his mind had passed. When the musicians arrived there was a stirring of worth; a brief span of time that stood still; allowing him joy in his wife and his children. The words to old songs were a healing balm. Sometimes the neighbors urged him to sing in that fine voice that spoke of toil and sorrow, peace and contentment, while they sat listening and nodding heads.

The children were watched by their mothers while the men worked the magic of the instruments and Julie often wondered why it was the thrumming of the guitar and the strain of the violin moved the people from tiredness to a happy murmur of gladness and appreciation for life. That was when John Buchanan loved his family most. Those were the times he carried Mark high on his shoulders and said, "This is my son, over there is my daughter. We are so glad all you folks could make it."

Chapter Three

Then it was July. July brought berry picking, down in the woods beyond the house. Julie watched the pickers from behind the shed as they moved from vine to vine. The Negro nannies wore bright three cornered scarves on their head that brightened the landscape. Sometimes she could see the scarves when she couldn't see the nannies. She'd asked John Buchanan about them.

"They're a proud people, little girl. Don't ever forget that. Their skin may be darker than ours but they are good people and they've been through a lot."

Wondering out loud, Julie voiced, "How would he know?" She wasn't aware her grandma stood within hearing distance that day. Grandma seemed to be everywhere keeping an eye on Julie.

"Was that sass, Julie?" Sass to Grandma meant she was being disrespectful.

"No, ma'am. I just don't know how daddy knows so much."

Myrtle Buchanan relaxed on her way to sit in the shade breaking the ends off green beans. "He knows, because he lived pretty much the life they have. We had nothing except each other."

"Julie," Sarah couldn't hear their conversation as she called from inside the house. "You stay in this yard and you watch for snakes. Cotton mouths own this swamp."

It was hard to believe. Theodore and Zac ran barefoot in and out of the brambles, scratched places on their legs and bled red blood just like she did. She'd been curious about that, them being black. She questioned Grandma, while she stared at Mark's blonde hair.

"Bloods blood, missy. You hear tell of blue blood in people of royalty. Ain't no royalty. No blue blood. They are just people born under different stars."

"We got any royalty in our family, Grandma?"

Myrtle raised her body, letting the ache between her shoulders ease from stooping over the scrub board that morning and then picking beans with Sarah. "None I can think of. Maybe on your Momma's side. Her family had that fine white house with thick carpet on the floor. Real carpets made of wool and her Poppa had that shiny black suit he wore on Sundays." She sighed, looking off into the distance. "He had a gold chain stretched across his vest and a nice black brimmed hat." Reverence tinged her words. "I always wanted to see that pocket watch up close that was on the end of that gold chain. I bet it was seventeen jewels."

"What about Daddy's poppa?" Julie's voice pleaded. Sometimes Grandma wouldn't speak about him; just like she wouldn't speak of the dried rose wrapped inside a piece of waxed paper hidden inside her Bible. She watched as Grandma stared into the distance, seeing things Julie couldn't see. Feeling an ominous presence, Julie waited.

"Him?" Grandma's voice hovered there in the past. "Looked just like your daddy. Taller. Had a way with words." Her voice slowed, like a tired old clock. "It was the Irish in him. His family brought him here, all the way from Ireland, when he was one year old."

"You loved him, didn't you, Grandma? Just like I love Daddy. More than black berry pie or my little duck before the horse stepped on him. It's just an ache inside since he's gone." Julie's vice grew quieter, her expression wistful. "I know you loved him."

"Hmph." Myrtle snorted, scornfully. "Him? Coming around long enough, and then leaving to do *his* work. Come with me, he'd say and I'd laugh. Not a joyful laugh mind you. How could I follow him around the country with six boys hanging on my skirt?"

"Why would you do that, Grandma? Didn't you have a house?"

"Yes, we had a house, young lady. A house with cracks in the floor so wide the snow dripped inside in the winter. The roof leaked in the summer and I feared snakes would crawl in while I slept and wasn't keeping watch." Myrtle rose up. "I'm rested a bit; I'll get back to that wash tub."

Following, Julie hoped for more about the Grandpa she had never known. She watched as Myrtle Buchanan scrubbed the clothes in wild abandon against the rub board. There was something desperate in her actions. Julie couldn't decide if Grandma wanted to cry or was angry. Talk of her husband had that effect on her. She seldom showed affection to anyone but Mark though, Julie knew as Momma said, *your Grandma puts up with you, Julie, girl.* And she coerced Grandma at every turn but today with her face stiff and foreboding Julie thought it was better to let the subject rest. Grandma's slapping the clothes on the rub board had to mean something.

Alone. Myrtle Buchannan paused for a moment seeing Julie wander off. She meant the child no harm. It hurt, remembering. She'd been alone, raising six sons on her own. Now they lived in Michigan, working in the plants, except for John and he resented the fact his father had never been around, blaming her. His child-hood voice stepped into her memory. "You could've gone with him, Ma, then we'd been like the other kids, we'd had a dad, too." But he had no concept the worry of that thought; staying in other people's homes, thanking them for the scraps off their table when she could do better on her own taking care of her brood. It was his father's fault but she got the blame.

Julie forgave her, for all the brisk ways she dealt with her own granddaughter, but then once having the same conversation she'd asked. "Wasn't Grandpa a good worker?"

"For Heaven's sakes, Julie, we were speaking of blood, Theodore's blood. It's as good as yours or mine. Maybe a working man's blood is a little better, who knows? Theodore's daddy works hard, those mules dragging him along, jumpin' stumps. I've driven teams before and it's not easy."

"Still, it would be nice to have royalty in your family. I wish I had blue blood."

"Great day, Julie. Wishes are fine, but wish in your own realm. If wishes were horses, beggars could ride." Myrtle Buchanan turned her back side to Julie. "No more talk, young lady, you go check on Mark."

The late September days passed slowly, a whispering quiet lay upon the land. Julie sat at the end of the day on wooden steps which led up to the porch. Trees were turning, their leaves scarlet tipped while Momma's garden thirst for water and Daddy's crops matured toward fall harvest. The shelves in the pantry were filled with Mason fruit jars bearing names of crops harvested and canned. Peaches and the date were on a label and Julie wondered why when clearly anyone could see the content.

Momma was precise in many things. "Please place the fork on the left side of the table." She reminded Julie and Grandma. Grandma would bluster and say she forgot while Julie secretly thought Grandma probably had never learned the true manner of setting a table and was embarrassed to say so, but then Grandma had worked for a famous French tailor and knew all descriptions of sewing.

Marigolds flared by the yard's edge. Orange. Julie savored the word. Orange. Nothing more, nothing less, just orange. Occasionally a breeze ruffled the fringe of bangs on her forehead, hot and aromatic it stirred the complacency of her world and she wondered that a wind could start at one end of the world and make its way to where she lived. Leastways that's what John Buchanan said and he read a lot, everything he got his hands on, her school books, bits and pieces gleaned here and there always reading in his precious spare time. She cast an eye to the South hoping there would be a cloud.

"White clouds of promise," Daniel once said, knowingly; his Daddy's words, no doubt. Daniel would thrust his body forward and use other people's words, making them his own. Commenting her thought to Daddy, he'd replied, "Perhaps Daniel will be another Red." Julie laughed, with understanding. But Grandma, being present had taken the opportunity to relate a story concerning clouds from the Bible.

"Once, it didn't rain for years," she began. "Three, I'm thinking, because the people were so wicked. God decided to punish them by letting their land dry up." Julie asked why. Daniel seared her with a scornful look but she knew he didn't know either. "Because the people's king Ahab was sinful; he and his people forgot the one true God and worshiped a foreign god named Baal. After three years of punishment God spoke to his prophet and promised to send rain which would correct the famine on the earth."

"What's a famine, Grandma?" Daniel seemed relieved she asked.

"When something is held back, like the lack of rain and the earth became so dry all the crops dried up. People became hungry." She's explaining for Daniel, Julie thought. Grandma never had time to tell her fairy stories but she loved to tell Daniel and Mark about the Bible. "Don't fill your head with such nonsense of fairies and the like," she said, more than once. "I once knew someone who did that."

"King Ahab had many prophets," the story rambled on, to Julie's way of thinking. "Those prophets carried out the king's belief in his false god. There were four hundred and fifty of them while Elijah was one man speaking against them, standing up for the people against the evil king." Glancing to where Julie's mouth was forming another question, she explained "Prophets tell people what God wants them to know and what he expects them to do."

"The people were confused wondering which god was stronger. Elijah told them to build an altar, to lay their sacrifice and wood for a burnt offering upon it. The four hundred fifty prophets were ready and their god didn't answer. They leapt upon the altar crying for rain and cut themselves with their own knives hoping their god, Baal, would answer." Grandma leaned forward to spit snuff juice a good distance beyond the porch. Daniel's eyes went wide in amazement, his eyebrows lifted nearly to his hair. Julie laughed silently that he didn't know Grandma's secret. Momma was ashamed of Grandma's habit of dipping snuff and asked Julie not to brag to her friends; still, Julie had to laugh when she saw the expressions on their face.

"It's bad enough that nasty can sitting around," Sarah fretted. "If only she'd put a lid on it to keep the flies out, but we don't have to spread this news, do we, Julie?" *No, ma'am.* "I don't know what we'll do when the baby starts walking. I guess that will be your job, Julie."

"But nothing happened," Grandma was saying, her eyes on Daniel. "Then, Elijah built his altar to the one true God, using twelve stones to represent the twelve tribes of Israel. He was so certain his God would answer he had the people pour twelve barrels of water over the wood. Water ran around the altar in a trench." Daniel leaned forward. "Elijah called upon the name of the Lord our God." Grandma's voice raised a pitch. "Fire of the Lord fell from Heaven, consuming the sacrifice, the wood and the stones and lapped up the water in the trench."

Daniel gasped. Julie wondered, was he interested in Grandma's telling of the story or was it the spitting? He seemed to watch Grandma with undivided attention. Maybe he could learn a thing or two.

"Then God said to Elijah, go up to the top of the mountain and wait for rain. When it didn't rain immediately, Elijah became impatient. He kept sending his servant to check on the clouds. Finally, the seventh time, the servant said, *there's a little cloud*. In time the Heavens turned black with clouds and wind and there was a great rain." She expected Daniel to get up and do a dance he was that enthralled.

Remembering, Julie grinned foolishly. She just knew after that day Daniel had tried dipping and spitting and you couldn't do one without the other. Now she glanced up at the sky. In the south there were a few clouds, maybe there was the promise of rain. For now she basked in the golden sunlight, with baby Mark sprawled in the playpen behind her, snoring gently. She didn't think she or Mark had sinned but she did wonder if adults sinned.

Honey in the bee- baw, bee- baw, bee -baw I can't see -yaw, see -yaw, see -yaw. Across the way, Zac and Theodore's voices drift to her ear. Somewhere deep in the woods they were playing hide and seek. Momma didn't allow her to go into the woods. Baby Mark wiggled in his play pen, sweet and damp waking from his nap. Julie giggled. "It's not such a bad world waking up to, is it baby Mark?"

That year in the fall, Julie and Daniel started to school, walking three miles each morning and evening. They struggled in the beginning learning to read and print but by Christmas an ease settled in their hearts as they practiced for a program. Julie would sing a song and Daniel would quote a poem. But it was the *hawg-killin'* in February, that brought all the excitement. Families arrived from all around, parked rattling cars and trucks on the side of John Buchanan's home; ready to do business together as they prepared food for the year ahead. Women scurried about carrying dish pans and sharpened knives as they exclaimed how cold it was outside.

Julie waited for the startup of the fire beneath the big black kettle. Daniel paced the yard, eagerly watching as the first hog was killed and strung up on a high scaffold. Stepping closer he watched as they scalded and scraped the hair off the body. It was an experience he would never forget and the flow of energy from the people sent shivers down his spine to see them all working together, talking and teasing each other until the day ended with everyone tired but happy as they bid each other good bye.

Little Mark had stood on tip-toe at the window wanting to be outside. "Don't you worry, son," Grandma comforted, pulling him to her side. "You'll be old enough one day to walk the yard with Daniel."

It interested Julie to see Grandma always comforted Mark, while she spoke to Julie through tight prim lips. Now she said, "You watch your brother, young lady. See that no harm comes to him this day or I'll hold you directly responsible. You've had your time outside, all ready, now you stay in and watch Mark."

Julie stared belligerently. "Why do you like Mark better than me?"

Myrtle Buchanan laughed a brittle indignant laugh. "You got foolish ideas, girl. Nobody likes one better than the other. Some just need more attention and you are the older." She left the room, but Julie stood rooted to the spot, her eyes glaring as she looked after her. She knew better.

Daniel had grown tired of the slaughter. "What can we play?" He asked Julie, handing over authority.

"How about barber shop?" She took the scissors from her mother's sewing basket, placed a towel around Daniel's shoulders and clipped away, some places right to his scalp. He resembled Daddy's pig lot, when there were dried up mud holes here and there, except for Daniel it was missing hair. Mark loved it, toddling through the cuttings on the floor, sputtering when it hung on his tongue.

The spanking wasn't so bad. Baby Mark sat on her lap and wailed, though no one laid a hand on him. He denied his loving privileges to all, comforting Julie. But that night the Black Panther ran through the community leaving huge paw prints down the rutted road. Zac and Theodore's parent's lingered by John Buchanan's side nervously watching the woods beyond their house. Neighbors had gathered and shook their heads silently.

"Judging by the distance between foot prints, he appears to measure near nine feet, more when he was stretched out and running. We've heard it before, but never thought we'd see it in our time."

"What's a panther?" Theodore whispered to Julie.

John heard the whisper and dropped down on his knees by Theodore. "What's troubling you, son?"

"What's a panther, Mr. Buchanan, sir?"

"It's like a big cat, fierce and wild, hunting its prey by night. Last one we had attacked the mules and livestock. You children are going to have to stay out of the woods playing hide and seek. Is that right, James T?" His gaze rest on Theodore and Zac's poppa. The little dark man was shaking his head.

"Tha's right, Mr. Buchanan." Theodore leaned in closer to his poppa's side. He felt his insides quivering, it was like a warning.

While the men discussed whether to take guns and hunt for the panther, Daniel slipped in between Julie and Eudora, Theodore's sister. "How'd your daddy learn about the leopard in time for warning?"

"Some man came last night," Julie explained. "Then we all heard its scream as it ran through."

"It was awful," Eudora explained. "Screamed worse than a mad woman. I'll never forget."

Julie pondered the excitement of the men, nervous and not knowing what to do.

Chapter Four

"Well, Jorney, guess you've heard. Your landlord turned his daughter out, without a cent, said he was disinheriting her."

John stopped what he was doing, stared at Red. "Which one was it? Annabelle?"

"That's right." Red was rolling a cigarette between his thumb and forefinger, bringing it to his lips, licking the outside before he struck a match to it. "Annabelle, the one with the yellow hair."

"The reason?" John glanced Julie's direction where she sat straddle- legged on the porch rolling a ball against the side of the house. Maybe she couldn't hear.

Red rolled his eyes, knowing John would be interested, when he heard. "Yeah, she had a wood's colt, so old Fritz turned her out."

The ball rolled off the porch. Julie ran after it, strolled around the house out of sight and crept nearer.

"Seems to happen in the best of families."

Red laughed his ridiculous snort of a laugh that made the sides of his over-all open where the slits were always unbuttoned to show bare skin. Stooping over he picked up a pebble and tossed it across the lawn. It landed near Julie's hiding spot. Staring at Red's gaping over-all and not a sign of underwear; she understood what she'd heard Momma say. "He's too easy, John, to be around children. Ours."

"Wonder whose it is," John asked.

Red grew quiet. "Up to speculation, heard tell." Both men eyed each other, nodding. "When you moving?"

"Soon. Got to tell Fritz. Have to give up the section."

Julie recognized the *section* to be land John Buchanan farmed for Mr. Fritz.

"What about the teams?" Red settled his back against a post and began to move to scratch an itch.

"I'll take them to Halfords to sell."

"All of them?"

"Most. Won't take as many with two tractors."

Red whistled low under his breath. "Poppin' Johnnie's. The sound of them old engines can be heard for miles. What about the black families?"

John sighed wearily as if the burden rest on his chest. Leave it to Red to bring the matter to daylight. "I'll have to leave them, too. They got to have enough work to keep their families alive. It's all I can do right now to keep them busy. They've been stackin' brush. I'll give them all good recommendations to the new man." John studied his friend. "Progress is never easy, Red."

"Jorney?" Red moved away from the post, looking John straight in the eye. "I believe I'll be movin' on."

"You're leavin', too, Red?"

"Think so. Hear there's work to be had in Kansas City with higher wages and less hours."

"Can't blame you, Red. I'll miss you. You're a good friend."

The two settled on an old saw horse, a shyness intermingling between them as Red's cigarette smoke circled above their heads. They seemed to stare out to the woods. Julie stared too. Annabelle's wood colt, was out there with the Black Panther. Julie shivered. She tried to imagine what a woods colt looked like, maybe black and shiny with yellow hair like Annabelle's.

They were moving, away from the grove of oak trees, the tool shed where she plaited water grass in smooth braids, moving to another house with smaller trees and a barn that spread out on both sides. "There's a loft to store hay," she heard her parent's conversation. "Julie will love that; she'll find a way to hide from your mother when she gets too bossy." Maybe she could take Daniel there when he visited and Eudora and Theodore, who would still be on Mr. Fritz place, there on the gumbo land that had been a swamp and was still over run with cotton mouths. New ground, she'd heard it called and it was said her daddy cleared it all. Mr. Fritz is going to miss John Buchanan, was the story Theodore told her.

They drove to the new place and Julie had her own impression. It's a big old chicken yard, she thought, all fenced in with wire that rose higher than her head and a chicken house with a slant ladder that led up to boxed nests. Daddy had been busy. Winter wheat spread a green blanket across the field behind the house. "We'll double crop," she heard him say. "It's the best I could do, Red. I promised Mr. Fritz I'd seed his place first and I did though it almost worked me to death, so much to do, both places."

"It'll be all right, Jorney." Red grinned. "Never seen you fail in anything, les it was that time in Anna." He brought light to his friend's eyes as he'd known he would. Slapping John on the back he continued, "I'm going to help you move then I'm pullin' out. I guess you done well, still tradin' someone else's land to farm your own, one section here you got to pay for against Old Fritz land you paid rent on." He scratched his head. He'd seen the worry in John's eyes. The man was too tense. Fearin' failure he'd worked his body thin in order to swing the deal. He had the mind of a pure bred stallion, high strain; a worrier and Red had always been able to bring laughter into his life, now he was leaving too.

"You need to let up, Jorney."

"Can't."

"Why can't you?"

John studied the ground. "I was twenty years old in nineteen twenty nine, more interested in raisin' a ruckus than anything else. A man has to eat, though, doesn't he? I got a job; worked with this old man tilling his soil, walked behind a pair of worn out plug mules whose bones showed through dull old hides; they were like staves under a wagon tarp.

John glanced up, a quizzical expression on his face as he shook his head. "I thought the old man was a fool, nothing to look forward to, even the government didn't guarantee him his crop would sell if he produced it." Glancing at Red he continued, "I went to Arizona that winter to work in the fruit groves. Thought I had a better chance but farmins' farmin', there's just different kinds."

"I know, Jorney."

"I came back the next year, worked for the same old man. We laughed about it. You know what he told me?" Red shook his head. "He said, John, even if you don't make money, if you love the land it ain't half as bad. Reckon I've always remembered that. It's a hard life. My shoes had holes in them. I stuck cardboard in for soles and poor as the old man was and poor as I *was* I stayed. By nineteen thirty two Congress created a giant loan agency to help since conditions were so bad and we thought help was on the way. But few farmers around here received any of that loan money. I was ready to give up when the old man's health began to fail. *Farm my land, John, he said, and if nothing else comes of it, I'll buy you a new pair of shoes.* He helped me get my start. In '33 the Farm Credit Act established a Farm credit system to lend short term loans to farmers, but of no help to me. It was already June. I wasn't approved."

Red laughed. "Luck of the Irish, Jorney. Did he buy your shoes?"

"That was no small fee." John grinned and nodded. "It took about ten bushel wheat to buy a cheap pair of shoes. Farmers talked about blocking their farm products from the market hoping to make prices rise but no one was brave enough to do it, couldn't afford to."

"Why'd you stay, Jorney?"

John laughed. "By then I was hooked. Like the old man said, if you love the land it ain't half bad."

"Guess that's why I'm leavin', Jorney. I don't love the land."

John turned toward Julie, "Come on, little girl. Time to go home and we need to drop Red off at the store. You can buy some candy, if you like."

Julie jumped to her feet. She wished Mark was along but Daddy said he was too little. She watched the ground slide beneath the truck as they rode along, the hole in the floor board by the shift left it visible. Now she glanced to daddy. How she loved him, wide shouldered with hair the color of copper her momma called it auburn and eyes the color of a bright blue sky. When they stopped to go into the store, he handed her a nickel with a buffalo imprinted on one side and an Indian on the other.

It was the road grader man stopped Julie as she followed John Buchanan. "Hey, little girl." Julie glanced up. Her father had stopped and was staring at the man, a strange expression on his face. "Evening, John. Here you go, girlie. Take this nickel and buy yourself some candy."

He pressed the coin into her hand and Julie didn't know what to do. "Thank you," she said moving to her father's side. Red and John exchanged glances. The road grader man moved on to his machine.

They walked through the double doors, the smell of sawdust and oil lingering in the air as Mr. Bingham swept the floor with a big wide broom he placed against the wall as he greeted them.

Standing at the glassed in cabinet, Julie stared at the variety of hard candy, aware the store keeper, Red and her daddy were having a private conversation. They left the store with Julie clutching a small brown paper sack filled with candy in her hand; two nickels definitely helped. But that night as the family settled into bed she heard her father say to Sarah, "you need to explain to Julie about taking gifts from strangers."

"She rarely goes anywhere with me," Sarah replied. "Since I don't drive." Her mother's voice was very quiet.

"You know about Eudora?"

"Yes," Sarah replied. "Another woods colt."

"Red heard the Caterpillar man was around."

"Red would hear that."

"Mr. Bingham confirmed the gossip. Loneliness does strange things to a man." John replied.

"No decent man would hurt a child."

"Time will tell." John yawned as the bed squeaked and he turned toward the wall. "James T is a sad poppa. He told his kids to stay out of the woods."

Moon beams streamed through the window as Julie strained to hear the whispers. Little Mark's body was etched in silver as he lay in his crib on white sheets. Julie peered through the metal posts wondering, another woods colt, Annabelle's first, and now Eudora's. She didn't understand Momma worrying over snakes; it was the Black Panther in the woods, and now the caterpillar man whose hair was black as a ravens. The real worry was in the depth of the woods.

So it went. Myrtle Buchanan moved into town; four miles away from the new place, where each day she wore a clean apron over her dress, walking the distance to the post office to see if there were letters from her sons that lived *up North*. John had remodeled an old house and made a comfortable home for Sarah and his children. The move meant a different school for Julie and Daniel's parents were leaving the farm for factory work in the city. Life was changing and Julie wondered if she would like it. One thing was different, even though it was rural area, there was electricity. Word had it back in the grove where they'd left the swamp land gumbo it would be another five years before tall poles went up and wire was strung taking electricity into those homes.

Life was changing and there was nothing she could do but go along with it.

It was going to rain. The cerulean sky had darkened around bits of clouds and quickly turned to dun. The trees were beginning to move restlessly from side to side, swaying near to breaking as the wind rose. Julie hurried at first, glancing anxiously at the sky, remembering Momma's warning never to stay outside nor under a tree when it was lightening. Lightning flashed in the south, coming closer as its jagged tail touched the bluish line of trees that stretched across the horizon.

She knew something was wrong the moment she stepped upon the porch. Voices beyond the screened door rose and fell. The undercurrent of mumbled incoherent words built and grew as the height of the storm approached now with white lightening flashing up from the ground.

Hesitating a moment, as a flash seemed to close in on the rough board planks of the porch she sank to her knees; the old swing was slapping against the wall dreadfully near the glassed window of the front room. As afraid as she was to be outside in the storm, Julie feared entering the house. She pressed against the wall, straining to hear. It was Daddy and Grandma.

"Lord, God, woman, it's been ten years." Her father's anguished voice rose in agitation. "You let me believe that all these years?"

"You will not take the Lord's name in vain," Myrtle Buchannan snapped, her voice rising.

"More like a prayer, woman." His voice roared. "How could you do such a vile thing to a man's sons?"

The wind whipped Julie's skirt around her legs and pushed her back, causing her to lose her balance, even as she knew her father stepped across the floor. She heard the smash of a fist on the small stand table and the scatter of her mother's vase breaking into pieces. High in the sky there was the crash of thunder and the jagged strand of lightening danced across the fields, scaring Julie into moans as she ducked her head and brought her fist to her mouth to drown out the sound. Mark yelped. Julie knew Sarah offered soothing tones of comfort.

"Ten years, Ma." John Buchanan's rage pounded in her ears as the rain came in huge drops making a white sheet beyond the porch roof. "Ten years you let me believe my father was dead."

"Who told you this?" Myrtle demanded, "You tell me who brought you such word?"

"A courier from town, of all people," John countered. "Is that why you're here, today, Ma? You already knew and you thought if you were here I wouldn't hear?" John's deranged laughter sounded above the storm. "Can you imagine? I told him there was some mistake. My father has been dead ten years."

"No sir." John's voice sounded terrible in Julie's ears. "Are you John Buchanan? He said, this message is from Unionhill, near Newport, Arkansas. Your father was killed in a river accident early this morning. There are arrangements to be made. Your name was given as next of kin."

Sarah stepped to the door, peering out into the rain, scanning the yard and then from the corner of her eye she saw Julie pressed tight against the wall; fright paling her skin, water dripping from the ends of her hair and her shoulders shaking as her sodden dress dripped onto the boards. Stepping out Sarah grasped Julie and pulled her through the door. "Why didn't you come in, child?"

"I was scared, Momma," Julie shook, her words coming out in stutters that wouldn't stop while tears ran down her face until she was snubbing as Momma's arms tightened around her.

"It's always so, isn't it, Julie; always bickering, two people alike not able to love each other in a peaceful way." Sarah's lips pinched together, her eyes slipping into a resigned gaze, "will it never end? Who will be next?"

Sarah hurried her past the two locked in anger; if they noticed her, neither so much as glanced Julie's way. Sarah toweled her dry, gave her a cup of warm milk and led her and Mark into the bedroom. Usually quiet, Sarah had an anger of her own. "They're like two animals at bay," she said aloud. "Cowered and waiting, one won't give in to the other. Listen to them, Myrtle hoarse, John pitched." Her eyes turned a violet shade of blue as she snapped the covers between deft fingers and pulled them up around her children's bodies. "You stay in here and rest," she said and Julie would never understand if her mother was speaking to herself or in a state of unrest completely unaware she spoke at all.

It was not hard to hear the rest of the story. "You came back from your trip," her father was saying. "You appeared one day with a letter in your hand. Remember that, Ma? You said he's dead. Not a tear in your eye, your voice cold and hard. He's dead. He died on the river. And you lifted the stove lid and threw that letter into the fire without letting me read it."

Myrtle Buchanan started to speak. Her son interrupted. "No need going," you said. "It's been two weeks. Everything's been taken care of, but you didn't let me read that piece of paper and I believed you."

"A piece of paper?" Something in her grandmother's voice alerted Julie. No more muffled denials. "Would it comfort you? *That piece of paper?*" Contemplating her son with scorn, she asked, "What about me, all those years left behind to take care of our sons, taking in washing for twenty five cents a day. Couldn't he get a job close to home, be there for all of us and you stand here angry at me over a piece of paper?" Julie tiptoed to the door and peeped through where the door didn't connect.

"It was my right to know. Paper or not. He was my father." John's eyes blazed with anger.

Myrtle stared back, bitterness churning in her soul. "You hungered for a father, begging me to forgive him all those indiscretions, all the times he went away and the things you never knew. How could I, son? He left us. Then, as surely as now when you've learned, he's truly dead."

"It was my right. I could decide on my own about my father."

"When you were twenty," Myrtle sighed, sinking onto an old chair. "I went, to be with him. Good intentions, mind you and mainly because you wanted me to. I didn't have to worry whether you boys were fed or not, you were all grown and gone, so I went."

"With your bible, you spoutin' scripture," John accused his mother, "I never knew if you believed it or not. Now I see you for the hypocrite you really are, leaving an old man to die, alone."

Myrtle pursed her lips, staring coldly into her son's face. "Who said he was alone?" She came up off the chair, her face inches from her son's. "Watch who you call hypocrite, son. It can turn on you; you're not through with life, yet."

"Sometimes I wish I was. Times like this it seems everything's against me." John was suddenly seized with despair, it dragged his body down, his soul, his mind. "Now there's a funeral expense and we've got to go make arrangements."

"I'll not be going." Myrtle's reply came quick, resolute and firm.

John stared into her face, bewildered. "But, he's your husband." He felt every ounce of strength draining from his body.

"He was my husband. He alone changed that situation. I've known no other man."

"It's your duty, Ma."

"That's a dirty word, son. What was his duty to us, to me?" She saw the dark shadows beneath John's eyes; out of six this one was his father's image. But this one cared for his family, in that he was different.

"If you don't go, Ma, don't explain why we've lived this lie all these years, don't talk to me in the future."

"So be it."

Wanting to hurt his mother, John considered what must have been in the letter. "You signed his death, you know. Ten years ago you said he died in a river accident. Does it comfort you to know he died as you said?"

Sarah listened to the discourse between the two. Did it occur to John he owed anything to his mother who had seen him through childhood. Not at this hour, she concluded. He was a man whose father had died alone, unloved, unwanted while his sons believed him dead ten years. Did he sit there with dark thoughts battering his mind, filling recessed alleys from childhood longing, hope and desire to have a father's love? Was he in some reasonless way determining no woman would hold power over him or would he turn to her for comfort concerning things he could never understand, a grown man with a child's hurt?

Sighing, Sarah waited, in the make shift hall, reluctant to return to John and his mother. What did Myrtle Buchannan mean, who said he was alone? No woman would share a husband willingly.

Julie hovered beneath the summer sheet, feeling Mark's small body comfortingly near. Fragments of the conversation flashed through her mind. Daddy's loss was her loss. "I hate Grandma," she said as the trembling ceased but the chatter of her teeth remained.

She hadn't known her mother was back, checking on her babies. "Why do you hate Grandma, Julie?" Sarah leaned across the bed, her gray eyes luminous as she questioned softly.

"She kept our grandpa from us, all those years," Julie whispered. "I'd hurt if I didn't see Daddy."

Sarah eased onto the side of the bed, laying a caressing hand on Julie's cheek. "Grandma hurts, too, Julie. When you grow older, you'll understand."

This was a new experience for Julie, Momma explaining Grandma. *Momma Grandma's ally?* Though she'd never heard Momma oppose her, she'd thought…

Sarah kissed her children on the forehead, left the room closing the door behind. She knew now that the rain had quietened, as soon as it ran its course, John's mother would leave to walk the four miles to her home. What had this day wrought? Tiredly resigned, Sarah drew the broom from the small closet. She must clear the broken glass from the floor. It mattered not, the vase had been her mother's.

"Tell me a story, Julie. Tell me about when I was born." Mark would ask then he would plead.

"Once upon a time, not too long ago," Julie began, "there was a baby born. A little boy and his parents named him Mark. He wasn't much to look at, kind of red and hairy."

"Oh, Julie." Mark protested.

Grinning, Julie said, "His skin was the color of cream and soft as cat's fur. He had the strangest blue eyes, like the color of the sky before a storm, blue-black and they looked right through you. This baby was happy because his Momma and Daddy loved him…"

"And his sister and his Grandma," Mark interrupted, in his chirping little boy voice. "He was little and his sister was bigger. That's right, isn't it, Julie?" Solemn eyes smiled upon her. "Go on, tell me about the promises."

"Julie." The call came from the kitchen. "I need you. Now."

"Not yet, Julie," Mark whispered. "The promises."

Dropping down to gaze into Mark's eyes, she said, "And he had all the golden promises waiting for him, because he was only four years old and had a long time to grow up and everyone to love him."

"Julie."

She thought Grandma wouldn't come around, and she hadn't. "She is letting the hurt settle between her and your daddy," Sarah explained. John had left for Arkansas the day after the storm, to meet with his brothers and make arrangements for their father's funeral the next day. On the third day, Sarah placed straw hats on her and the children's heads and taking their hand begin the four mile walk into town to see Myrtle Buchanan. "You must play outside, quietly, while I speak with your grandmother." Her gray eyes held them in firm understanding they were not to question but do as she said.

A knock brought Myrtle to the door. "Mrs. Buchanan," Sarah addressed her mother-in-law, "Are you all right?"

Myrtle's laughter was hollow as the tingling sound of a chime in the wind. "Why wouldn't I be?" She seemed pleased to see them. "Come in. Come in."

"The children will play outside."

They settled into facing chairs. "John will come around," Sarah began.

"No, he won't." Myrtle stated matter-of-factly. "Make no mistake, about that, Sarah. He won't."

"Surely," Sarah's gray eyes wore a painful expression. "Surely…"

"No, Sarah." Myrtle replied softly, a firm rebuke. "Never think it. My only regret is…" Myrtle stared out the window. "I don't want this coming between you and John. I know sometimes I'm a bone of contention, as it is. You're quiet, Sarah, never complaining about my interference but John's full of wrath."

Sarah started to protest. "We…"

"Shh, girl. You think I don't know? But this time, he doesn't understand, Sarah. Maybe you don't either." Blue eyes turned a troubled gaze upon her. "A man doesn't understand how it is to be carrying a child, all those months carrying with the fear it won't make it or if it does that something might be wrong with the baby." She peered into Sarah's face. "Something could be wrong because you did this or that, trying to take care of your family, maybe the old mule kicked you and you fell against the side of the barn and no one was there to help you up and you wonder and wonder if everything's all right…" She clasp her hands tightly together, remembering. "That's how it is. There's the good moments full of anticipation but when you're alone they don't come as often as the fear." She sighed, a heavy searching sigh. "Alone. That's how it was. Most years. He'd come around, long enough to get me with another baby. Then he'd leave. Another job, he'd say. Come with me. We'll find a room." She lift her head, a contemptuous gleam in her eye. "A room? Five boys in one room? A room?" Her laughter was brittle.

"The real hurt came when I was carrying Hattie. He never even knew he had a daughter." Her voice softened, "Until she died." The ache was like a cloud in her eyes. "Nine months he didn't check on me. Gone the whole time, one letter in between. Work's not good, it read." She laid her head back against the chair, for a moment staring at the ceiling. "I knew. Me, doin' washings for other families and I was heavy with child. Maybe that's what went wrong, my liftin' all those heavy tubs." Pain fluttered there, behind her hand over her stomach, pain in her eyes that Sarah could see.

"She was never healthy; Hattie, our only little girl, a golden child, tiny, sweet and bubbly." Myrtle felt intensely weak from the telling. "I should've known. Something warned me from the beginning. She did everything too soon. Quicker than the boys, she sat alone, cut her teeth, walked, everything early, toddling around those boisterous boys, an angel in the midst of hellions. How we loved her. The boys carried her around like she was a princess. I was able to dress her better in clothes given to me often in exchange for a day's work, mind you, whereas the boys had tattered hand me downs. Nothing was ever free. Golden. That's what she was. And then she died, from the fever, the doctor said. Fever."

"And he never saw her," Sarah questioned, gently.

"No." Myrtle stood to pace, twisting the apron she wore in her hands. "Never." She brushed at the corner of her eyes with the apron. "A woman doesn't forget things like that and a man doesn't understand.

"John understands. Just give him time."

"No, Sarah. He never understood. True, he was young but there were all the times he insisted I keep tryin' with his father." She went to the window, looking out on the children playing. She saw the past and the present. "That last time," she paused, "I went a week earlier than planned, after John saw the letter where his dad ask me if I'd try again and Johnnie begging and pleading I go." She slipped into her son's boyhood name as she faced Sarah. "I arrived too early. He had a woman with him, there in the room. I saw too much and it all came sweeping over me. I got on the train and started home." Sarah hung her head knowing what followed.

"The letter I burned in your stove, Sarah, the letter John didn't read, was his dad explaining the situation. *I was wrong he said, letting you find me that way. It meant nothing but I was never sure you'd come. Come back. It will be different.* He was dead to me. I wrote him a letter, in it I said; you're dead to me John Buchanan. Dead. If you come around us, I will tell our sons all the things they don't know."

Sarah raised her head letting her gaze settle on the older woman. "If only there was something I could do."

"There is. Just forget you've heard this."

"John's so upset, if I could explain part of this," Sarah groped for words.

"I know my son, Sarah," as if contemplating him sadly, Myrtle continued, "For now he blames me but the degree of self-doubt will come when he questions why he readily believed what I told him ten years ago, but pride will never let him accept what he knows in his heart."

Sarah called to the children. "Let's go home; your daddy will be there soon."

"Sarah," Myrtle called to her daughter in law, "Remember, John said we'd never speak of the matter again."

In the following days, when his mother finally came around, John ignored her, his body as tense and tight as the strings on his fiddle. Myrtle, speechless and grave faced, helped Sarah when need arose. They are alike, Sarah thought, too stiff to bend and the strain pressed a spot around Sarah's heart.

"Momma," Julie called, "The mailman left a letter here for Grandma."

"It's from Arkansas," Sarah said, scanning the address, "I guess the mailman doesn't know she moved to town." She placed the letter on top of the cupboard. "Help me remember to give it to her."

From that month, until she died, Myrtle Buchanan received a small pension from the last place her husband worked. Her son wondered how she could accept the money. But Sarah understood. "You should be glad. As she grows older, she needs it and she deserves every penny, all those years she raised the six of you with little help from your father."

"What do you know about it?" He replied sarcastically, eyeing her with an angry glint. Sarah was silent, her shoulders firmly squared. John knew she had her own opinion. With his stomach on fire due to the conflict with his mother, he wanted none with Sarah.

Chapter Five

Electricity made a great difference in their home. It seemed as the oil lamps were placed on shelves in the smoke house for emergencies, other things begin to disappear. The familiar red check oilcloth used to protect the good oak table was folded and put in the buffet drawer on Sundays. Out came Sarah's mother's good white linen cloth with the fine lace edging. Myrtle Buchanan eyed the material with pleasure.

"When I worked for the tailor," she said, "He taught me how to make tucks and the many tricks to make a lady's dress; but it was the lace he added to his wife's garments I'll never forget. He used linen for the back ground and linen thread for its softness. One dress, in particular, was blue, periwinkle with blue tatting." Grandma's face softened as she brought the memory alive.

Even Sarah lingered in the doorway, listening to Myrtle Buchannan's accounts from the past, knowing there was always a question. "Did your mother wear pretty dresses, Sarah?"

Considering for a moment, "Not colorful," Sarah replied, "But fine material." A frown creased her forehead. "Yes, yes she did. But they were usually black or a navy color with tiny tucks and lace around the collar."

"I thought so," Myrtle nodded, satisfied. "I knew, because your daddy had that fine watch and suit."

Listening, Julie was reminded, sometimes she didn't think Grandma was nice to Momma as if Momma might take on airs, her family having more wealth, but then Grandma was remembering the periwinkle dress, wasn't she? She couldn't snap her son's wife's head off if she were the one asking the questions, now could she? Feeling she must stay on guard to protect her mother, Julie considered this new alliance between them and the time she'd asked her mother, "Why do you allow Grandma to boss you around…and me?"

Sarah replied, "Julie, girl, it is ridiculous for you to worry yourself over such small matters. Myrtle Buchanan knows more about life than any ten women I know put together. I've learned a lot from her."

"But she's so bossy and that time you let her slap me."

"Yes, she is that, but you sassed her and she didn't deserve your disrespect. Besides, Julie, who else do you know willing to help us prepare lunch for the hired hands, scrub those endless dirty clothes and be here for us?"

Julie would give Grandma that. As the seasons changed from winter to spring, there were summer's buckets of peas and beans to shell, and cucumbers and squash from the garden to put on the table. The women worked together, splitting the produce and seeming not to mind the work of putting it up.

Mark pestered Julie to tell stories as they sit shelling while the women canned. "I swear, Mark," Julie spouted occasionally, "You know as much as I do. Your background is same as mine. Wasn't it, Momma?"

"It hurries time." Mark glanced to where his mother was loading jars of vegetables, knowing after standing all day her back and legs ached. "It's different, too, and Momma's back… what you called it is too."

Lifting sealed jars from the cooker, on the stove, Sarah paused a moment, a fleeting memory of the two story white house stirred in her mind with sounds and smells from long ago. Her parents were both gone but sometimes the memory poignantly ripe brought an ache to see them into her heart. What will my children remember, she wondered. "It's true, Mark, our lives may differ but some things remain the same."

"I swear, Momma, I don't think Mark has learned a thing."

"You can quit that swearing, young lady," Sarah chided. "And I don't think Mark's mind is clouded with fairy tales."

"I do that for Mark," Julie's words flared for a moment. "Of course, Mark, is caught up in Grandma's Bible reading. He can spout them scriptures, can't you Markie? Go on," she prodded, "say one."

"They that wait upon the Lord shall renew their strength. They shall mount up with wings like eagles. They shall run and not be weary and they shall walk and not faint."

Sarah's heart quickened beneath the faded cotton wrapper she wore, as she listened intently to Mark.

Julie laughed, "I like that, Markie. I really do. Wings like eagles. How come they don't fly?" Peals of laughter rang from Julie.

The swat of flesh hitting flesh brought Sarah to the door. Mark had punched Julie on the cheek. "You shut up, Julie, makin' fun of God's word. Grandma says we mustn't do that." He glowered at his sister.

Julie rubbed her cheek, tears smarting in her eyes. "You little twerp. Don't you do that again. Grandma needs to teach you something else. That's wrath and God don't like wrath, either."

"You shouldn't laugh at God's word, Julie." Tears glistened on Mark's eyelashes. The anger faded as quickly as it had come. Seeing the red spot spreading across Julie's cheek, he threw his arms around her, letting his head sink against her chest. "I'm sorry, Julie."

She felt his anguish, the weight of his body, too. "It's all right," she soothed. "You like scripture. I like fairy tales. I'm sorry, too."

Sarah stepped away from the door. It was better if they settled it themselves.

"Give me another scripture, Mark."

"One thing have I desired of the Lord, that will I seek after, that I may dwell in the house of the Lord all the days of my life to behold the beauty of the Lord and inquire in His temple. For in the time of trouble He shall hide me in his pavilion; in the secret of his tabernacle shall he hide me; He shall set me upon a rock." Mark grinned. "Psalms twenty seven, verse four and five."

Julie stared at her brother. "Momma," she called through the door. "Isn't that a bit complicated for a little boy?" She frowned as she considered the words. "Do you know what it means, Mark?"

He stuck out his chin, as Sarah stood once more in the door way. "Yes. I do. It is about war and enemies, but though a host encamp around me, war rise against me, if I have the Lord, I won't fear." Mark's grin spread across his face. "Grandma explained it to me."

"Is that true, Momma?"

"Get the Bible, Julie. Read for yourself."

"If it's true, Momma, how come Mark understands and he's younger than me. It's a lot of words."

"Maybe he's special blessed, Julie." Sarah didn't know. The boy did seem to have an understanding. She felt it. Mrs. Buchanan said she'd never let him memorize anything he didn't understand, but the older woman had concluded, 'out of the mouth of babes comes perfect praise and understanding.'

In his innocence being neither arrogant nor boastful, Mark said, "I'm going to tell people about Jesus when I get big."

"What can a boy possibly tell older people," Julie scoffed but she was interested in Mark's answer.

"Grandma says there's a whole bunch of people out there who haven't heard the story of Jesus. They're lost because no one takes time to tell them. I'm going to, Julie. Grandma says I must if that's what burns in my heart."

"You're too little, Markie, boy." Julie snickered. "After you tell them they're lost, what then?"

"I know more scripture, Julie."

Julie's mind had traveled on to other things. "What about the war in Korea, Momma? That's where two of Daddy's brothers are, Grandma said so. Daddy said Eisenhower promised to bring the war to an end, that's how he beat Stevenson. It was on the news."

"Campaign promises, Julie. They all make promises. You seem to understand the news."

"Daddy explained it. He says the Democrats control the government but Eisenhower is a Republican."

"I don't understand politics, Julie. It's all I can do to can these beans."

"Will Mark ever have to go to war?"

"I certainly hope not. Everyone hopes the war will end soon."

"We could go together," Mark interrupted.

"Girls don't go to war, do they, Momma?"

"Why not?" That puzzled Mark. "Do they, Momma?"

"Sometimes."

"Do black boys like Theodore and Zac go?"

Julie laughed. "Sure they do. Eudora said her oldest brother went. Why wouldn't they?"

"Zac said we don't want them in our schools, maybe we don't want them in our war."

Accustomed to hearing the evening news, John settled into the chair, turned the knob on the radio and listened. His brothers had chosen careers in the armed forces. Now the news commentator droned on. "The Korean war seems painfully inconclusive for Americans who wish to think in terms of victory. The war in the last three years has cost the United states twenty five thousand lives and one hundred fifteen thousand recorded casualties, not to mention twenty two billion dollars to prevent the communist conquest of South Korea."

"What a price to pay," John sighed.

"The money, Daddy?" Julie asked.

"The lives, little girl."

Pushing a toy truck around the braided rug, Mark looked up, questioning the burdened sigh. Everyone spoke of the war but when he looked around outside, everything was the same. He couldn't see a change and he wondered what the grown-ups knew that he didn't. Then one day his father brought home a small wooden boxed instrument with a receiver he placed on top of the house. Now Mark began to understand, in black and white pictures flashed across the screen of the television bringing terror to his young mind and for a while to his dreams.

Julie felt the unrest of world in her father as his attention was drawn to the news. She felt his concern to the extent she sat each evening by his side to listen to the news and tried to understand the worried look in his eye. Mark was drawn to the room because his father and Julie were there. He listened, not understanding but letting the words roll through his mind, coming often to the tip of his tongue. Then, in the spring of 1954 the United States announced that its government had exploded a bomb powerful enough to destroy a city the size of New York. "In retaliation of enemy countries who have threatened the security of the United States," the commentator explained.

"What's retaliation, Julie?" Mark asked. Julie looked to her father for the answer.

"When one government has something and the other must have it too," He answered quietly. "That keeps one country from being more powerful than another."

"What for?" Mark whispered to Julie.

"I guess to keep countries from making war?" Daddy was so intent listening she wouldn't bother him.

"But, Julie, why do we keep having war?"

"Because people like to have control over each other."

"Well, I don't want to control anybody," Mark concluded. "Where's the war and daddy's brothers now?"

"Listen, it will tell." Their father was giving them a look that said be quiet or leave the room. Julie knew. She had the conversation with her daddy too many times, though he tried to be patient with her.

"President Truman has asserted the United States continual support of the French military effort in Vietnam as foes to the spread of communism in Southeast Asia. It is estimated more than seventy percent of the cost of the French effort in Vietnam will be paid for by the American tax payer."

John Buchanan uttered one word as the commentator's words ended with one press of the button. "Vietnam."

"I don't want to go to war, Julie."

She patted his shoulder. "And I don't want you to. Let's go get your bath and help Momma. The cotton choppers come tomorrow."

Mark was considered half-a-hand at seven years old, as was Eudora's boy who was younger than Mark but considerably larger. "Where's your big brother, now?" Julie asked.

"He living in Chicago, just like everyone else I know."

"Why Chicago?"

"That's where the money is, in the factories."

They chopped in silence, the click of metal hoes sometimes heard as they slashed weeds away from the cotton. Julie was always painfully aware of Eudora's woods colt, now that she knew what it meant.

"Does it hurt, having a baby, Eudora?"

"Yes, it hurt something terrible. My Momma say next time won't be so bad, that I was young with this one." Eudora laughed, slapping her thigh suddenly, "You remember that time we come to see your momma and poppa to show them how Zac and Theodore had grown? You said, what happened to your wood colt, Eudora." Tears ran down her brown face as she stood for a moment, laughter seizing her again. "I said, you dumb, Julie. You so dumb."

Embarrassed, Julie remembered. "Yeah, Zac and Theodore pointed at the new baby. Until that moment I thought the baby was your Momma's." She stared at Eudora., remembering Eudora's baby could pass for white with his soft mulatto skin and silky black hair. "It's a wonder you don't have another." Julie still wasn't exactly certain about the pros and cons of two people birthing a child.

"Poppa said it better not happen again but Momma said I was so tore up havin' this un, she doubts they'll be another."

It had taken Julie forever to figure out the wood colt situation, then last month a letter arrived from Daddy's friend, Red saying he was bringing his wife and children back to see them if it was convenient to John and Sarah. That day, Daddy sat down and wrote the letter telling them to come on.

She didn't know who was most excited as the shiny black automobile arrived and Red stepped out to grab John Buchanan, the two friends patting backs and Red lifting John off the ground in a bear hug. "Meet my wife, Annabelle," Red said proudly, "and my son, Richard and our little girl, Marie."

Annabelle? From the stirrings of her mind, the name haunted Julie as she examined the boy named Richard, while Marie had red hair, Richard's hair was black as a ravens and Annabelle's hair was yellow. Marie was toddling toward the flowers by the door step, while Richard lingered by the automobile. "Come on, boy," Red beckoned, explaining to John, "This one's too shy, for his own good."

"Annabelle." John Buchanan was saying, "Sarah, you remember Mr. Fritz daughter, don't you?"

Julie sighed. There was a mystery to growing up. The sun was rising higher in the sky and Eudora was a good pace ahead as she had slowed trying to sort Eudora and Annabelle having their wood colts that she now understood turned out to be little boys. The two had a strange resemblance and that worried at her mind. How could it be? There were things not easily explained.

Chapter Six

Mark wasn't particularly impressed with school, but he went giving no trouble. He made friends easily and it didn't matter whether they were black or white, and if a black boy needed defending it would be Mark standing firmly by his side ready to do battle. As he grew, Julie found him many times playing hard with his friends, tiny droplets of sweat on his upper lip and she would tousle his hair as she passed by knowing Mark realized it was a gesture of affection.

John hired a helper and when times became fraught and his nerves on edge he would slip away, taking Sarah, to go fishing. Mark loved to fish but on those occasions John said, "No, son, not this time."

Bill, the helper saw his disappointment. A jack of all trades sort of man, Bill seemed to know how to do anything the farming operation required. He and his wife, Letty moved into a house down the road with their son, who was a few years older than Mark. In time, Bill arrived every day ready to attempt whatever job needed doing. On the day Mark was denied the fishing trip, Bill said, quietly, "We'll go when it rains, Mark." And they did, Bill, his wife Letty and Joe Lynn. Sitting in the shade of a cottonwood tree on Number Five ditch was good enough. It became a happy spot to catch catfish and no one was against the nibble of sun perch to keep their attention.

Grandma had reduced her visits to once a week, still working with Mark teaching him the scripture and explaining passages that made no sense to Julie, but Mark seemed to understand. Myrtle was often tired after the walk to the farm. "Many stop and ask me if I want to ride," she told Sarah, "But John don't like it. He says I'll get knocked in the head." Looking exasperated, she stared at Sarah. "For what?"

Overhearing, from the porch where he'd stepped in for a drink of water, John appeared in the doorway. "Ma, you shame me. "If you'll send word, I'll come get you."

"By the time you get word, I can be here." Bridling, she said, "I just want to see the kids and how the crops are growin."

"You are too old to walk four miles."

"I do it, don't I?I could handle your cotton choppers too, if you'd let me."

John would shake his head wearily. "No thank you. We've had this discussion before."

Myrtle arrived one Saturday morning while Sarah was preparing dinner. It was Myrtle's way, after many encounters in the small kitchen, to leave cooking to Sarah while she set the table. Sarah had called to the children to come in and wash their hands with John soon to follow, when she suddenly dropped the heavy lid of the iron kettle. They all heard her anguished cry as it landed on her foot. She stood staring at the floor as pain ran up her leg and her big toe languished in spasm. Sweat popped out on her brow as she saw the heat of the lid eating away at the linoleum's veneer and steam rising.

"Sit down, Sarah," her mother-in-law demanded, pulling Sarah toward a chair. "We'll soak that foot in Epsom salts to reduce the swelling."

"Under the sink, both," Sarah replied, easing the shoe off her foot as Grandma examined it, then rose up to fix an Epsom salt bath in a square pan from under the sink.

"You'll probably lose the nail." Grandma's hands were in the water, gently massaging Sarah's foot. "No broken bones. But a good size whelp."

Mark had seen the purple knot rise up and the pain on his mother's face. "Let's go get Aunt Effie. She'll know what to do and she'll bring the prayer cloths."

"Prayer cloths?" Myrtle eyed Sarah and then turned her head to study Mark. "What's this about a prayer cloth?"

"She sent away for it, Grandma." Mark leaned in to peer into Myrtle's face. "She told me. Somewhere in radio land the man said you lay it on people with sickness and it heals their bodies because someone prayed over it."

Standing, Myrtle forgot Sarah. Taking Mark's hand she led him to a chair where she sat down and pulled him in front, looking directly into his eyes. "It's faith, son. Do you understand? It's not the cloth; it's the prayer and what another person believes. I've told you about that."

"Can you do it, Grandma? Can you pray and make the pain leave Momma's foot?"

"No, I'm not sure I can. That's not my gift and it takes a lot of faith, the laying on of hands."

Mark's chin protruded stubbornly. "I'm going to have it, Grandma. I'm going to ask God to give me that gift. When I'm big enough, I'll just ask Jesus. Aunt Effie believes and I can, too."

"That would be wonderful, Mark…"

"You know what else, Grandma?" Mark was standing firm. "I'm going to speak in tongues."

"Speak in tongues?" Grandma cried out, "Lord have mercy, Sarah. What do you mean letting your son around that woman? She'll have him converted to her belief in no time."

"I'm not prejudiced to denomination, Mrs. Buchanan." Sarah wasn't overly concerned with Mark's religious choice at the moment with her toe throbbing blue blazes. "You've seen that Mark has enough scripture to last all his days, and we're raising him in our family faith but Effie's a good woman and if she believes that way, it's her right." Tiredly, Sarah closed her mouth and her mind as she studied her toe.

Mark wasn't finished. "Your toe looks like an Easter egg," he said as his eyes lifted to his grandmother, defiant and near anger. "It's in the Bible. By His stripes we are healed. Not that we got to do anything but believe."

Myrtle was taken aback, ready to have the last word. "Let me get the rest of dinner on the table, Mark and think about it, if the Bible says by His stripes we are healed, then we don't need prayer cloths, do we?"

Even Mark's believing didn't save him from a tonsillectomy. Swollen red with white spots of infection, the doctor said his tonsils must come out. Sarah and John prepared to leave that afternoon after the surgery, with Sarah promising to return the next day. With an overflow of patients, it perplexed Sarah that they would not let her stay.

"Good bye, ole rabbit," Mark said as Sarah kissed him goodbye.

"Now why did he say that?" Julie asked.

Sarah smiled. "It's his way of being brave. He's a little boy afraid but he doesn't want us to know." She looked into the distance, her mind years ahead. "He's my brave boy and will always be my baby." His early childhood days were filled with play, but the seed of insecurity had been planted, a thing neither he nor Sarah understood but the root of it was John's irritability. By the time he was eleven, Mark knew without a doubt his presence had become a problem.

John excused himself as an overly tired and overworked man. He couldn't put his finger on why the boy got on his nerves, asking too many questions, not understanding the answers in John's short clipped sentences. "I had no one to explain things to me," he said. "I've been on my own since I was fourteen. Sarah, the boy needs to settle down, leave the playing behind." John had joined the church after giving his heart to the Lord. He thought it would make a difference in his rash disposition but it hadn't. All he could do was ask the Lord for forgiveness.

It was another Sunday when the pastor gave the altar call "If there's one here who feels the tug of the Holy Spirit stirring in your heart, come forward. Let your soul be saved from the eternal torment of hell." His voice swelled with the magnitude of leading others to Jesus. "People let us pray for these who find it hard to walk the aisle. Let us pray God gives them strength and courage as they walk the aisle, Dear Jesus, wash their sins away, as far as the earth is from the sky, to the far ends of the world, Lord, wash them. It matters not the age. If you know right from wrong, if you feel a burning in your heart, then you know it's time you give your heart to Jesus."

Julie glanced across the aisle. Just as she expected, Mark stood between Momma and Grandma, his hands gripping the pew in front, eyes closed, as he shifted weight of his body from one side to the other. The pastor prayed through, "amen." Grandma opened her eyes to glance at her grandson and saw the troubled expression on his face. Then, Grandma met Julie's stare, and shook her head gently.

Myrtle had been told, the last Sunday after the altar call as they hurried home for lunch, Mark asked Julie, "Why is the preacher talking to me? Why doesn't he look at someone else?"

Julie had laughed. "He's talking to everyone. Not just you." Disappointed with her reply, Mark hung his head. "You'll know when it's time for you to go forward, Mark. You won't rest until it's done."

She saw him reach for his mother's hand, then Grandma's. Both women smiled as Mark stepped out into the aisle and walked forward to meet the pastor. "Praise God," the pastor's voice boomed. "A child's name shall be written in the Book of Life." He stooped with his arm on Mark's shoulders, to talk with him, and then he was preaching again. "All you have to do is believe in the Lord Jesus as your Savior, repent and be baptized. Ask God's forgiveness. Repent and be baptized. Mark Buchanan has come forward to make a statement of his faith in Jesus. He has repented, ask forgiveness and we wait for your acceptance of him into our fellowship and most importantly to the Kingdom of God."

And as Mark stood before the congregation, his friend, Joe Lynn went to stand with him.

"I never seen a child so bent on learning the word," Myrtle said to Sarah. She cut her eyes to John standing near, "I know, you thought it was me pushing him to learn scripture but it was Mark, himself. He's got the understanding. Sometimes I think Mark will receive calling to the ministry."

"I hope not," John replied. "That would be no life for a boy raised on a farm with all its freedom."

"Worse things could happen," Myrtle admonished. "I'd think you'd be proud of your son."

Mark listened, recalling the many times his mother said of his father, "He doesn't feel well, Mark. Try not to worry." Together, they would stare out the window. "He says it's the pressure of living, I don't know why exactly, but there's little I can do to change his thinking." Considering all the other daddy's he knew, Mark realized they laughed and played with their sons but the last few years it was as if the life was being sucked out of his father. Even Momma with all the work she did smiled as she worked in her roses.

It came to him there was a stage of life beyond which his understanding could go. You knew it was there but couldn't explain a painful restraint that bound your heart and soul. Sarah's gentleness had a calming effect but he wondered if one day his father's impatience would hurl itself between them in some terrible reckoning. As surely as dark clouds gather before rain, the cloud of concern hung over Mark's head. His Grandmother realized the problem and believed it was because her son's own father was absent in his life.

"I know you are too young to understand, Mark." Grandma would gaze off into the distance as she explained. "But there are circumstances where husbands and wives cannot stay together. Mine was that your Daddy's father left too often. He was a wanderer who called himself a carpenter. I could not travel the road he chose with six boys hanging on my apron strings. In spite of it all we survived but I do not know why your daddy's spirit was so broken when the other five flourished with health."

Trying to nap in the adjoining room, John knew they thought he was asleep. He felt tired and overworked. He had envisioned a better life for his family and by some standard he had done better than most. He and Sarah survived the depression with their love intact. But ma's unsettling lie had nearly destroyed him; that terrible need revealed in the light of day that he had desired a father all those years as much while grown as that pitiful bare existence he'd known as a child void of his father.

"Do you think he cared?" She'd asked, her eyes blazing with temper to match his own. How was he to know? He'd not been allowed his father. "There are few hurdles a parent will not cross if they love their child." Tossing on the bed, sleep would not come as thoughts hurled themselves mercilessly. He didn't know how to respond to his own son. It was a silent war. The boy expecting something he didn't know how to give. "It's your fault, Ma," his conscience whispered. He closed his mind, trying to sleep, trying not to think, depression taking hold, destroying the strength of the daring man he had been in the past, to become a shadow of himself.

The drone of their voices ebbed, as his eyelids closed, wavering to see a tall man, his image, broad shouldered, laughing and playing a violin, his mother smiling briefly, the smile turning into a painful shattered countenance as the tall man left, taking his music and the joy they'd known so briefly. Gone through the bleak days of winter when they scrambled to find fire wood, stuffed paper and cotton into the cracks of the wall. With his brothers whispering out of Ma's hearing they wondered where he was, their Poppa; hoping he would return and sometimes he did a year later with a bag full of candy, wearing a new coat and hat, his face shaved clean, to stay awhile and break their hearts when he left again.

He awakened to the quiet of the house. The restless spirit reminded him he was a man of the church now. The pastor's sermon brought the demons to life; that invisible thread of worry, why he and Mark had no relationship, wondering that Sarah was always in easy conversation with their children. Surely it would come, but when? Teaching the boy to work was a bone of contention. John wanted things done right, his way. Was this his thorn in the flesh the minister spoke about in his sermon?

Observing, on occasion, Myrtle chided him. "You use your son as a scapegoat for everyone else's failures."

"Woman, you are out of your mind. The boy must use that thick head on his shoulders if he is to become a man." The question rose again, silent taunting, why was he at odds with the world?

"He'll be a man we'll all be proud of," Myrtle declared, spitting juice a good three feet, knowing John waited for an excuse to barrel into her verbally. "You got something to say, get it over with."

Sarah overheard, wondering that the tension flared between John and his mother same as with father and son. Mark deserved better. He was a child, turning into a young man and John was sick, the ulcers of his stomach spewing acid into his system. He glanced her way, his eyes filled with anger. "What?"

"She's right. Mark will never be thick headed. But he's not called to the soil, he doesn't have your love for certain things but he does have an understanding in many areas which you do not." She spoke quietly, always gentle but her words carried a sting that went straight to John's heart.

"Hoot Johnson's boy can drive a tractor and has since he was seven years old."

"Don't compare Mark to the Johnson boy, John. That boy's father took him with him everywhere he went since he was two years old. You did better with Julie, in that respect, but you never expected her to drive a tractor."

"Life changed about the time Mark came along. I was busy."

"You had no patience." Sarah stood her ground. "Mark wanted to go but you wouldn't allow it."

"A man has pressures," John replied. "What does a woman know? A man has to make a living."

"Admit you're wrong, John Buchanan, let us get on with life before you turn our son into a nervous pup."

"Enough." But Sarah's words turned in his mind like a windmill in his head round and round. Was she right? He truly didn't know why he felt such a loss. Maybe it's your fault, ma, his thoughts whispered.

Beyond the house stretched long rows of cotton. Julie was halfway through the field when Mark picked up his hoe by the smokehouse. His face was swollen from crying and the whelps hurt where the shirt touched his back. He stared at the green plants, thinking again of the green limb in Daddy's hand, void of leaves it had slapped at his back cutting tiny ribbons of flesh until blood sprinkled purplish spots on his skin. Waiting until his father left, he stripped the shirt off, craning his neck as far as he could to see.

"Cry." His father cursed, landing yet another stripe on his son's back as he demanded the boy cry. "Twelve years old and ran that tractor off in the ditch. I ought to beat the mischief out of you. What you got rollin' around in that empty head of yours, boy? You got too many grand ideas."

It hurt when his mother, rubbed ointment on his stripes. Out of her husband's sight she placed her arms around him lovingly. He turned away, stone faced, his body unyielding. She'd seen enough pain in one day. No need her seeing the hate in her son's eyes. He waited until his father left to cry bracing the tears with scorn.

"I can't drive the tractor, Mamma," his voice rasped. "Daddy won't take time to teach me and I don't know how." She'd found him. He'd thought he was alone, but she'd come looking for him.

"Shh. Shh." She comforted. "He's a good man, but he's impatient. You're just a child trying to do a man's job. He should've gone for the neighbor in the first place," she soothed "But son, if you'd cried he'd stopped. I know you felt like it."

"But he cussed me, Momma." Flinching as she touched the deeply torn skin, Mark's body trembled. "He tore the limb off the tree and said, keep walkin' across the yard, boy. And he beat me as I walked. Why does Daddy cuss me, Momma?"

Sarah's face looked pinched and shrinking for a moment. Then her expression softened, "He never had a daddy, son. Maybe he doesn't know what a father is supposed to do. You go on now. Chop cotton with Julie before your daddy comes back with Mr. Eaton." Her words faded as Mark walked toward the field. "They'll get that tractor out, son. Don't you worry."

He was a good boy and how he'd grown. Built like his father, the wide shoulders, the square chin protruding with its air of stubbornness, the similarity of the bright blue eyes; but there it ended, his was not the temperament of John Buchannan with the fiery disposition and the auburn hair. No, Sarah considered, Mark was more like her brothers, quiet and gentle with a deep searching way; a boy of twelve reading scripture.

What she thought meant nothing to her strong willed husband. But this time she'd thrown her body between the two and she'd do it again. "Hit me, John Buchanan. Lay the lashes on my back, for I swear by God's goodness I'm as guilty as this child."

He had drawn his hand; she saw the prominent veins in the muscular arms that knew so much labor but he'd not laid a hand on her. This time he'd gone too far. While she realized the tiredness settling in his bones and knew the financial strain concerning the farm was desperate she'd have no more of that. It was not the fault of a child the tractor was in the ditch. Mark hadn't brought the rain.

She was a silent woman wearing the serious gray eyes, uncomplaining as she wore flour sack aprons, never looking in the mirror, thinking herself a simple woman. It would have surprised her to know the community thought Sarah Buchanan a beautiful woman, inside and out. With her olive skin and dark hair, Mark might have been built like John Buchanan but his resemblance to Sarah was profound in his love for the Lord.

From the kitchen window Sarah glanced now and then to where her two children worked. John had told James T he wouldn't need the crew until the next day but Julie and Mark were sent on to the field, the soil sticking to the bottom of their shoes and the hoes as they walked along the rows of cotton. Such was the situation, weeds trying to claim the plants and John remembering years when they had, due to too much rain. John had taken the tractor to the end of the turn row and slid into the ruts, but when he had Mark on the second tractor to pull him through, Mark's tractor had slid into the ditch.

Chapter Seven

Not given to outburst, Sarah felt the problem between her husband and her son shadowed their lives and robbed their joy. It was her duty to see that Mark did not wear the scar from childhood his father wore. The gray eyes became more serious and watchful as Mark walked the path down to Joe Lynn's house, where her son and his friend could rough house or sit and talk with Letty and Bill, feeling their love and understanding over things he dare not speak in his own home. She ached, wishing Mark were there that moment, when it seemed he was all she had to keep her going from day to day. But wisdom ruled and Sarah knew she must turn loose and let him go. She smiled when Letty related the boys singing. "You'll hear them on Sunday, Sarah. Joe Lynn loves that song The Ninety and Nine."

Julie was another matter, she moved between them all, listening, comforting her brother, biding time. She would marry the boy down the road who found her to his liking. Julie's temperament had changed, she no longer felt the urge to rebuke her grandmother; the two had grown close with Myrtle teaching her crocheting while Sarah taught her all the other intricacies of running a home. And Julie loved her father, sensing his need to be loved in a way no one could fill. Sarah recognized her daughter's discernment and wondered that this spitfire of a child had come this far. Sarah moved within the boundaries of her home, filling need, wondering in old age what would be the cries of her heart. For now, the world was opening up for her children, soon she and John would be as alone as when they first began.

The marriage was posted in the local newspaper. There was a flurry of Bridal showers and Mark watched, grinning as Julie turned, from the sassy girl who dogged their Grandmother's path, into a lady of sorts. Even Mark was surprised what Blaine's love for his spit fire sister brought out in Julie. And Mark loved Blaine. No one had ever taken as much time to talk with him and listen to questions as Blaine. He watched his mother preparing for the reception at the church, wondering with all the added work that she could seem happy in the midst of such activity. Relatives were invited. New clothes for himself and his father were purchased and Sarah's dress hanging on the door to the bedroom was nothing like she had worn before. Pink in a soft fabric she called *shantung*, he knew his mother would be beautiful. His father had assumed an air of gruffness. Mark wondered if perhaps he was sad with Julie moving the short distance away and the thought did occur if his father would feel sadness or relief when he left. Then he noticed John Buchanan was humming a tune. "Why's he singing?" He asked his mother.

"Could be he approves of Blaine. He's always said it will take a man to handle Julie." Together, they laughed. "Come with me," she said. "There's the church to decorate and you can help."

"Where's Grandma?"

"She's already there. Hurry now, your dad is driving us down. Julie will bring us back."

Myrtle met them, carrying a long white bag. "I got this dress through the mail, Sarah. Will you see if it's appropriate?" She lay an arm around Mark's shoulders. "I can't have Julie ashamed of me, can I?"

Everyone said it was one of the prettiest weddings. Mark didn't know because he'd never paid attention to any others but John Buchanan was said to have done well by his family and hearing that

Mark wondered that the social prominence of a man was judged by his daughter's wedding. Still, his father in the black suit, his own a replica and his mother in that fluff of pink *shantung* was a picture. But it was Julie in the white wedding gown made Mark proud, she reminded him of a princess. "Little seed pearls," grandma explained, "hand sewn all over the gown right down to the long train that followed Julie down the aisle." She had paused beaming with a glow on her face that made her look younger as she continued, "That's the finest lace. Julie will save that dress for her daughter to wear someday. And look at your daddy, doesn't he look grand? He does, and Julie is a princess." Mark agreed. On this day there was an abundance of love and Mark felt proud.

"You look pretty good yourself, Grandma." Mark claimed her arm. Grandma's dress was cornflower blue, she said, of a good gabardine fabric and the collar was linen with a staunch Belgium lace. Mark shook his head, wondering at what women had to remember. But he loved Grandma; it was all right.

After Julie married Blaine, Mark happily spent the weekends with them. A teenager now, he was thrilled with the attention Julie's husband gave, the wise instruction and patience as Blaine taught him how to drive the tractor and explained endless matters that Mark thought would make a difference with his father. There were occasional movies and fishing trips when the three laughed and loved being together.

Frank was the colored boy who lived next door to Julie and Blaine. Wide shouldered, dark as night with dusky eyes and white teeth that glistened the many times Frank smiled; he and Mark became best of friends walking the distance two miles to buy candy from the country store or a bologna sandwich. It was amusing to Julie to see the two locked arms, wrestling until they rolled on the ground laughing and enjoying their friendship. Joe Lynn was beginning to run with older boys and Mark only saw him at church on Sunday. He knew John Buchanan would never agree to his joining them.

Sometimes when she visited home, Julie sensed the friction and asked her mother how things were between Mark and their father. "About the same," was the answer, or, "Not good at all this week."

Bill was not blind to the situation, either; Bill's son, Joe Lynn, and Mark were still friends and Julie asked his opinion. She thought wisdom shone through Bill's smile and listened as he spoke. "I don't know why it is," he said, "that your daddy and Mark have problems. Neither one of them want them."

"But it happens," Julie replied dully. "And Momma's in the middle. And there's no reason for it."

"No, not rightly," he said. "Many times your dad says to me, Bill, I wish me and my boy had the relationship you and Joe Lynn share."

"You'd never curse your son, Bill."

"No. And it hurts Mark when your daddy does. John's sorry later but he never tells Mark and he should. Your daddy bein' a Christian and all, that's his thorn in the flesh and he seems helpless with it."

"He could stop it." Bitterness crept in to Julie's voice. "I wonder what it's doing to all of us."

"I've worked here a number of years, Julie. That tells you your daddy is not a bad man. And James T's relatives that moved away up North still come every year to see your daddy and Momma. They think the sun rises and sets on your folks. Your daddy helps anyone who needs it. He ain't bad."

"You think Daddy loves Mark like you love Joe Lynn?" It embarrassed her to ask.

"I think sometimes people don't mean to get on each other's nerves but it happens. That don't mean they don't love each other. There's just conflict and they don't know how to deal with it."

"You don't have to say that if you don't mean it, Bill."

"But I do mean it. Julie, every man has a dream. Your daddy's was to have a farm and take care of his family. He told me he had nothing' as a child. You know things don't matter that much to me, me and Letty are content but your daddy nearly worked himself to death realizing his dream. He was driven. It 'bout near killed him. He's tired, Julie. But don't give up on them, it's never too late."

"What's your dream, Bill?" Embarrassed she spoke hastily. "You don't have to answer. I apologize."

"It's kind of hard to put in words, Julie. You know that little girl they said her parents kept her in a cage all these years and the authorities took her away from her family?"

"Because they moved off and left her and someone found her? It was in the paper."

"That's it." Bill scratched his head, thinking. "Me and Letty discussed that pretty good. You know what I wish, Julie?" His face lit up with pleasure. "I wish me and Letty had a big old house with lots of rooms and enough money to take in children like that, that have no one to love them and listen to them." Sadness entered his face. "We just don't have the finances but I guess that's our dream."

Julie drove home, wistfulness in her own soul that Bill and Letty could find their dream. She could see sunlight streaming through the windows, Letty in the kitchen making pies and Bill tending the garden with children following every step he made and at day's end they'd all sit on the porch. The children would nestle close and Letty would sing soothing lullaby's that made their hearts glad.

What had he said? "It will never happen will it?" Bill had scuffed the toe of his shoe on a rock. "Will it?"

Now she replied, "I thought you were the one who said it's never too late."

The seasons come and went. Spring rains made planting late and then farmers geared up for wheat harvest. Mark was with Blaine. "Can I drive the combine, Blaine? I've been watching you. I know I can."

"I don't know bub. You might hit something and stop the machine; a chunk of wood could break a few fingers off the auger or worse tear up the drag chain."

Disappointed, Mark slid back down by the seat, a cramped position but he wasn't complaining. "I guess."

Glancing quickly at the boy, Blaine explained. "It's not just the machine, Mark. It's a big responsibility on my part letting you do things. If you got hurt your parents would have my head."

"I doubt that." Mark wiped sweat from his brow. "I'm not that important, besides I've not told them you've taught me how to drive the tractor." He listened as the combine motor squealed. "What happened?"

"That's what I meant; a large clump of beans got stuck in the auger." He was aware of Mark shifting his body as he tried to get comfortable. "Why don't you go home and help your dad, Mark?"

"You know he doesn't want me out there."

Reluctant, Blaine stopped the machine, motioned for Mark to get in the driver's seat as he stood hunched over. "All right, bub, let's see what you can do." Excited, Mark hopped into the seat and waited with an upturned face for instructions. It was nearing dark when he drove the combine through the lane and parked by the tool shed. Blaine climbed down stiff legged to rub his back as he touched ground. "That was a killer, standing like that."

Mark hugged him. "Thanks, Blaine. It doesn't seem so hard when you tell me what to do."

A week later, Bill fell off the combine while tightening a chain on the clean grain elevator. He returned from visiting the doctor in a cast. "I can't bend," he apologized to John Buchanan. "I sure am sorry."

Julie and Blaine arrived as Bill was walking down the lane toward his and Letty's house but turned back when he saw Julie and Blaine and was ready for Julie's question. "What happened?"

Shame faced, Bill explained the accident. "I shore have let your daddy down," he said.

John was trying to figure the best way to fill necessary positions. "We have to get the beans planted behind the wheat. James T is coming to help, so he can work with the cotton. Maybe I can teach Theodore how to disc ground and that leaves me on the combine to do the threshing."

"I'm so sorry, John." Bill was wringing his cap between his hands. "I'm completely responsible for this."

Exasperated, Julie piped up. "For Heaven's sakes, Bill, you didn't mean to fall, did you? Stop apologizing."

Blaine listened to John talking with James T, who was saying, "No, sir, Mr. John, Zac doesn't know how."

"You have another option you aren't considering."

"What's that?"

"Mark could drive the combine." Blaine stated matter of fact.

Casting dubious eyes his son in law's way, John laughed. "He doesn't know the first thing about…"

Undaunted, Blaine continued. "Yes, he does."

"He's not like you were at that age, Blaine."

"I taught him."

The days of harvest were interesting to Sarah as she watched from her kitchen window noting John had relented allowing Mark to help. "He's not half bad with that combine," John admitted. "At first I was scared for him, me and the combine." John chuckled, pride in his smile. "I knew we needed no other problems, with Letty helping down in the field. Bill has insisted if he had someone to fill the planter boxes, he could manage planting back, behind the wheat crop.

Letty was helping due to Joe Lynn's absence. John shook his head, thinking they gave their son too much freedom. He was gone on a trip and here was Letty helping Bill so they would have a week's pay. He would've paid Bill, anyway, but Letty would receive payment for her hours as well. "She's a good worker but it's hard on a woman, that lifting." Sarah saw Letty, behind the truck, emptying seed into a bucket she carried to pour into the planter boxes. The pain around her heart had eased no doubt due to less tension between father and son.

Julie sat on a stool at the counter watching Sarah flip fried pies in the skillet. "I used to pray it would rain every Friday," she confessed. "Like if I didn't realize the rain just made the grass grow quicker."

"How're you feeling?"

"Fine. No morning sickness, though Blaine has been feeling queasy. Have you ever heard of the husband having morning sickness?" Sarah smiled. "Have you told Mark you're going to have a baby?"

"No. I will this weekend."

"He's going to ask questions."

"Oh, Mom, I told him about that long ago."

Sarah's face reddened. "You did? When was that?"

"About the time Eudora had that second baby."

"Julie, he was too young, then."

"Oh, Mom, Mark's not dumb. Kids know everything these days."

"You could have told me and saved me a lot of wondering, I learned the hard way. For instance, that Eudora's woods colt was her child."

Puzzled, Sarah took a chair across from Julie. "What in the world are you talking about?"

"When I was little I overheard you and Daddy discussing Eudora's woods colt, then in the spring when Eudora's brothers came to work for a while, I asked about Eudora's woods colt. I thought they'd bust a button laughing. I pulled authority over them," Julie grinned, "as Daddy's daughter, I said you either explain that or I'll tell you're not chopping all the grass out of your row. So they explained." Julie picked up her purse ready to leave. "You didn't tell me enough, Momma, so I told Mark what he needed to know."

"I bet you did." Julie was almost out the door when Sarah asked. "Julie, did you tell Mark how girls get pregnant?" Embarrassed, Sarah heaved a sigh. "I mean…well, he likes the girls now."

"Yes, Momma, I did and I told him to keep his hands in his pockets, just like Blaine did, until he's married."

"Oh, my word. I wondered how you handled the specifics."

"I drew him a diagram, mother." Julie was laughing as Sarah pressed a plate of pies toward her. "I didn't, but I will if you want me too." Julie's laughter carried as she walked to the truck. "Bye, Momma. I love you." Almost to the truck she called, "Thank you for the pies. We'll pick Mark up Friday night."

For some unknown reason, Sarah's thought went back to meeting John and then marrying him.

"It was a come-down for you, wasn't it Sarah, marrying Johnny." His mother had asked quietly. And she had looked quickly to see if envy or animosity was in Myrtle Buchanan's face. "You're a good girl, Sarah. Johnny's a dominant man and I know your folks were more genteel.

Years had passed, she supposed they had each proven them self. Now she worried over Myrtle. She'd seen the lengths of bleached muslin hanging to dry on the clothes line. Caught, with her defenses down, Myrtle showed her the large lump in her side, saying, "Dr. Hobart says I've ruptured something and I'm to bind it." Turning away, she modestly rearranged her garments. "It seems to help."

"See another doctor. Julie can take you. Dr. Hobart's only a country doctor."

"There's nothing can be done." Sighing, Myrtle explained. "I consider this trivial, Sarah. Women from my generation have many complications from childbirth. Mercy, Sarah, a woman that worked hard as me, driving a team of mules, it's a wonder I'm here."

By the weekend the rain had come again. Julie dropped by to pick up Mark earlier than she'd intended. Mark met her at the door, duffle bag in hand, ready. "Mom and Dad went to town for groceries."

"How'd the work go this week? Is Dad behaving all right?"

"Yeah, it was fine. Dad went to the doctor for a checkup, he said for the cancer he had years ago."

"Come on. I know there's more. Tell us." Mark squirmed under her scrutiny. Blaine grinned.

"It could've been worse." Mark knew she wouldn't rest until he told her.

Mark closed his eyes, pretending to sleep. Even now he could see his father standing on the ground, nostrils flaring, agitation causing his body to jerk impatiently. "Why's this machine stopped, boy?"

Mark sat on the platform, waiting. "There's a few fingers missing and Bill's gone to town for them. He said we better check the drag chain, too."

John grabbed the metal hand rail, swinging his body up onto the steps of the ladder. "You weren't watching, were you and forgot to raise the header over these mud holes, didn't you?"

Mark glanced back nervously. "I did. I really did." Step by step his father was coming closer.

"I'll check that belt and if you're lying to me," John cursed. "I'll beat the hell out of you."

Letty pushed open the door to the make-shift cab where she had sit to help Mark and Bill on the ground as they needed someone near the controls. "Meanin' you no disrespect, Mister Buchanan, sir," her lips pursed tight for a moment, "If you lay a hand on this boy, you might as well be prepared to beat hell out of me, too, Sir."

John drew back in surprise. "This is no concern of yours, Letty. I didn't know you were there."

"I reckon you're right, Mr. Buchanan." She drew herself to full height. "This child has done a good job. He's careful, because he's scared to death you're gonna' get onto him. Or, maybe threaten to hit him."

Eyes flashing, not one to be reprimanded by a woman, John replied, "You'd do better to mind your own business, not to spare the rod in order to spare your child."

She was taken back. She and Bill were proud of Joe Lynn, he might not know scripture like Mark but Joe Lynn loved to sing and John Buchanan had no idea those two boys were teaching the little ones at church.

Letty's mind pushed ahead, he was criticizing the way they raised Joe Lynn and that was none of his business if they raised their child with love and not all those grand expectations towards complete obedience. "You are speaking of Joe Lynn." Her eyes flashed warning, even if he bore a point; it was not his place to say.

John stared her down. "Your boy needs to learn how to work to make it in this world, Letty."

"You don't turn the tables on me, Mr. Buchanan."

"And you don't interfere where my son's concerned. It's evident he was not paying attention."

Taking in the white of Mark's face, Letty suddenly wished she'd not spoken at all. She couldn't place how it happened so quickly she had reacted without thinking. This was Bill's boss. Her voice lost volume as she said, "I'd think you'd be proud of him. He's done a fine job. Bill said as much."

"I'll take a look, Letty. Perhaps I acted a bit hastily."

Sometime later, seeing Mr. Buchanan leave the field, Letty moaned, "What have I done?"

"The gall of that woman." John stood in the kitchen. "Telling me what I must not do." He shuddered. "My life has been filled with interfering women."

"Wasn't it better than if you'd acted on your first impulse? The truth is you're upset because she heard you speak to Mark that way, not the fact that you shouldn't have in the first place."

"You lose the whole point. She interfered and I won't stand for it." He pounded a fist on the table.

The dishes jumped as the silverware she'd laid in preparation jingled together. Sarah eyed him coldly. "You lose the point. Letty merely pointed it out to you. Mark has worked hard and he's done a good job. It's a man's job. Recognize his worth. That's what Letty meant."

John shoved his setting toward the center of the table, dishes rattling. "You women stick together." He cupped his stomach as it churned in agitation. "No wonder men have ulcers."

"And women die of broken hearts."

"What does that mean?" He demanded.

"Don't make him hate you John. I'm in the middle. Do you consider how you treat us both?"

He laughed his terrible laugh. She ignored him. That didn't set well. He jumped to his feet, the chair falling backwards as his hand sliced through the air and sent dishes flying to land on the floor.

"Treat you? Treat you? Here, inside while I'm out there. You must be out of your mind."

"Where you want me, right John, unable to drive, dependent on you?" She studied her mother's dishes broken into pieces on the floor. Tears streamed down her face, as she said, "All this because you didn't handle things right?"

He couldn't bear Sarah crying. "Sarah," he pleaded. "My stomach's in turmoil. It's not worth it."

"You know what Letty asked me, once?" Sarah's gray eyes rest on him;. "She asked If you'd ever hurt me."

John turned visibly pale. "I never have." He sat down wearily in the chair intended for Sarah. "I never would."

"But you hurt Mark and it hurts me. The time you whipped him across the yard, do you think he will forget?" Her words snapped through the air. "You are killing us because you won't control yourself."

The retching came and he staggered to the bathroom vomiting blood. When his body was calm, he returned to find Sarah had returned his chair to its place. Their oldest dishes stained through the years replaced her mother's and Sarah sat in her chair, silent. She was all he had. He could walk through fire if he had Sarah. If she left him it would be like dismembering his body. "I need you," he whispered, tears in his eyes. "Sarah," he pleaded. "I don't know why it happens. It just does. I need you, Sarah."

"That is no longer enough," she said. Her voice unbending she watched him thinking how old he looked. A terrible loneliness gripped her soul as he slumped onto his knees and laid his head in her lap.

"I'll try," he said, the muffled words coming softly. "I'll try." Through the haze of his own tears he saw Mark standing just beyond the kitchen door, tears streaming down the boy's face and he wondered how long he had stood there.

Mark heard it all. Bill had not found the parts needed and sent him home, saying its quitting time anyway, Mark. He didn't know if he should speak. He felt their pain. There would be more times like this but tonight he'd seen a side to his father he'd not seen before. He dropped his head, keeping distance, afraid.

John stumbled to his feet, crossing the floor, extending his hand, reconsidering to withdraw it. "Mark," he whispered, hoarse and spent. "Forgive me, son. I was wrong."

Mark wavered, uncertain what he should do. Motionless, lifting his eyes to his father's face finally to put out his hands. "Dad?"

All John saw, was his eyes, blue, serious, he could have been looking into a mirror. His arms closed around his son, feeling the trembling of the boy's body, recognizing the squaring shoulders. His son was becoming a man. *Oh, God. Help me. I don't want to hurt him. Help me.* In that moment, he remembered the boy he'd been; wanting his father to put his arms around him, love him, never go away, never let the minute pass, fusion, oneness of spirit, *God help me.*

"Mark?" Julie touched his arm. "Are you asleep? Or just pretendin' so you won't have to tell me?"

As time passed, the bouts between Mark and John were less but when they appeared, the whole house trembled. Mark graduated and planned to leave but his father said, "I need you." His boy was leaving and he didn't know what to say to ease all the years of hurt and if it could happen all over again he wasn't sure it would be any different. The ulcer gnawed at him day and night, the doctor telling him he needed to find a new way of life. Then new test revealed cancer in his lungs. "We could operate, John, but that might make the cancer spread more quickly. You decide."

"How much time do I have?" John asked.

The doctor replied. "It looks like the cancer you had before has spread to your lungs, not farther mind you, not in the bone, but this happens. This type, cancer in the lung usually doesn't move as fast but it does create havoc with breathing. We don't know a lot about it, yet."

Appraising the sky, John thought there should be a happy medium in life; rain all spring, drought through the summer and the crops barely hanging on under the onslaught, like him. Then, the summer storm with sulfurous skies arrived, with rain beating out its wrath to soak the dry earth. He finally told Sarah.

"Sarah, it's my health. I don't want the family to know. I expect you to agree." She had agreed with a sad expression.

Myrtle had stayed away; her own health had become a problem though she remained silent on the subject. Her son was gaunt, his color off. Her grandson was quiet. "Where's the end to this?" She asked.

"Mark's ready to leave. There's a job in St. Louis but John wants him to stay. It's another dead lock." Sarah sighed. "What are your thoughts?"

"He still plans to marry that girl?" Sarah nodded and Myrtle thought for a moment, tilting her head, while a barrage of times past filed through her mind. "I hate to see him go, but if they love each other maybe it will be best."

Sarah turned away, her face ravaged with pain. "Why have we gone through these years of struggle, Mrs. Buchanan? Will any good ever come from it?" She wanted badly to tell her mother in law about John's cancer but he forbade it. How could she keep it from her children? John was their father.

"Why do women bear the brunt, Sarah? I don't know," Myrtle replied quietly. "Why do husbands turn against wives and sons their mother?" Sadness crept into her voice. "I have no answers but this I know, John loves his son and Mark loves his father, we can hope in time they work through the pain."

"Mark has said many times, he may not come back." Sarah sighed. "But that was in the throes of their arguments. I've become sick in my soul over the discord."

"Is Mark still helping with the kids at church?" Myrtle had dropped out of Wednesday night services. The walk stirred up the hernia in her side, in turn giving her sleepless nights. Now her neighbor brought her mail from the post office. She'd not told John or Sarah. They'd learn soon enough.

"Yes, ma'am, and there's a revival beginning this Monday night." Sarah considered Mrs. Buchanan's absence of late. "Will you be attending the revival? Joe Lynn's home. The boys may sing. Joe Lynn and Mark."

"How's the driving lessons coming along?"

Sarah's chuckle brought a smile to Myrtle's face. "That bad or that good?"

"I'd never have learned if not for Mark's patience."

"If you will pick me up, I'll go every night. I'd like to hear them sing. I thought Joe Lynn dropped out."

It was Mark's favorite scripture. "They that wait upon the Lord shall renew their strength; They shall mount up with wings like eagles. They shall run and not be weary and they shall walk and not faint." The words stirred within his soul as the pastor questioned, "Have you known thirst and tiredness when you thought you could not go a step farther?" He smiled as hands went up. "This verse is for you. Now let us consider the Eagle. We picture it soaring high above the earth out of the reach of man, broad sweeping wings, until it rest on the highest place it can find. It is said one particular nest found by men, was on a rocky shelf of a mountain. The nest measured seven feet high and six feet wide and it was surmised it would have taken two wagon loads of material to build that nest. How long would it take with a beak for arms to collect that much material? Can you imagine a wing span of eight feet and eye sight beyond our imagination with the ability to make a pin point landing by maneuvering its body successfully without a runway?" The congregation chuckled. "It would be good to have that strength when we are tired and weary, wouldn't it?"

"The promise is there. We can have that strength. It is the strength of a believer." His words drew them in. "Of all the literature of the Bible none surpasses the beauty and insight of Isaiah. He speaks to people in exile, comforting a people who lost all, telling them God, the master of creation, is still in control. Whatever the desert of one's soul, there's hope. God has a purpose for each life."

Mark listened, knowing the scripture, understanding. Sweat broke out on his brow. The word of God spoke to hearts and minds as the pastor read Isaiah. "Now, while the Spirit is speaking, while the Spirit is urging, do not turn away. God may be calling you into service. Rest assured, God is there in the plan."

Gripping the pew in front of him, Mark's knuckles turned white. He'd be leaving soon. Maybe that was what this was about. But he knew it wasn't. God was speaking to his heart.

Chapter Eight

John studied the center matched boards of the new floor. He'd laid them before the relatives came for Mark and Lauren's wedding. Myrtle watched him. She knew his thoughts. He would never voice them to her but he was struggling with Mark's leaving. Then, suddenly John was heaving, his breathing fast, and his color paling as he slumped into the first chair. "Where's Sarah? I need my medicine." Sarah had agreed, they would say nothing about the cancer found in his lungs no need to concern the family.

"I'd get it for you but I don't know where it is. You best find it yourself. Sarah's getting ready for the wedding." Myrtle didn't bat an eye. "I don't suppose you've noticed, Sarah's looking a bit peaked."

"What do you mean?" He rose up, one hand remaining on his stomach. "Why's she peaked?"

"Why have you been walking the floor today and finding numerous things to do later?"

Staring gloomily across the room, John replied. "I'm worrying, Ma, wondering how the boy will make out in the city."

"He'll be just fine; just like you, when you married Sarah."

"You think so?"

"You need to quit worrying, son. That's what's causing the ulcers, isn't it?"

"Yes, ma'am." But he grinned, not as sarcastic as usual. "Either that or some bacterial thing inside of my body." In his own way, he was calling a truce on Mark's wedding day but now he had Sarah to consider, whether she was sick or not when Ma called her peaked.

Sarah wandered around the house to her rose garden to stand staring at the mulberry tree where Mark had played. Tears welled up in her eyes. Hurt and joy mingled together; Mark seemed happy with Lauren in his life. Neither had dated much and when they found each other in tenth grade Sarah had watched the two unfold as a butterfly comes into its own. She and John had felt the magic and it reminded them of their own beginnings. Lauren had planned to attend college but as in love as they were she feared she would miss Mark enough that she would be unable to keep her mind on studying.

"I think I will get a job," She confided to Sarah. "Then, if I decide to go to college perhaps I'll be more settled to the idea." When she had become suddenly shy as they were preparing the table for lunch on a Sunday, Sarah stopped to study the girl.

"Is there something happening I should know," she asked. Lauren had extended her left hand. There on her finger was a silver ring with a small diamond in the center. "Are you two engaged?"

Lauren nodded, afraid what Mrs. Buchannan might think, since Mark hadn't told his mother.

"So that's what he's been saving for?" A smile brightened Sarah's face as she opened her arms to Lauren, but the smile dimmed slightly as tears brimmed her eyes. "I hope you will feel welcomed to our family," she said, "and love us as much as we intend to love you."

"I was afraid you'd be upset, Mrs. Buchannan, but it just happened yesterday. I really do love him."

As if a special blessing rest upon their heads, the sun had shone brightly, today, on their wedding. Mark now had someone of his own. For that, Sarah thanked God, as her thoughts turned to life with John, just the two of them when the depression come, no one to stand with her.

Splat. She heard the fall of the juice as Mrs. Buchanan spat and came to stand near her.

"Nice wedding." Myrtle saw the temporary wrinkle of Sarah's nose. "I waited til the guest left, Sarah. I know it's a dirty habit but it's my habit and I need it today." She studied the roses. "That yellow one, it's Peace, ain't it?" Sarah nodded. "You'll be all right, Sarah. I watched six boys leave home." She stared across the yard into the past where Sarah couldn't see. "It wasn't easy. Folks said, it'll be easier for you now, Myrtle, with less mouths to feed but it wasn't; a little piece of me went with each one."

Silent, Sarah considered her mother in laws words along with her dress. "Ain't wearin' black to the wedding," she'd said, "Black's for funerals. Ain't proper at a wedding; weddings should be a happy time."

Myrtle Buchanan was a handsome woman, wearing the small brimmed navy hat with its veil pushed back for daytime wear, sitting on the crown of white hair. She was neat and dainty, funny how Sarah was seeing this for the first time. Her mother in law was turning frail. She wondered about the stomach wrap for the hernia. What if it were not a hernia? But Myrtle Buchanan bore no interference. There were no blemishes on the woman's face, though she had worked in the fields and now endless hours in the garden wearing a long sleeved shirt and a bonnet to shade her face. Only the hands, wide nailed and wrinkled betrayed the many years of hard work. Past seventy, Sarah would have to count to know how many.

"I said, we're happy for him, aren't we Sarah?" A smile fluttered about her features. "We trained him well, didn't we?"

Sarah bowed her head as the tears trickled down her cheeks. Myrtle reached out to grasp her hand. "You don't mind my sayin' that, do you, girl?" Sarah's face crumbled as she shook her head. Myrtle reached farther, taking the girl that had married her son into her arms. "He's going to be just fine and happy, Sarah. You'll see. He's got that good job and he'll be home weekends."

"We're moving, Mrs. Buchanan," Sarah replied. "I'll be leaving everything I've known." And though she didn't say it, Myrtle knew she meant her, too.

John started around the house to find Sarah and suddenly he stopped in his tracks. *Well. Well. Well. Never thought I'd see the day Ma comforting Sarah.* Turning he walked back to the front of the house, muttering, "*Wonders never cease.*"

Often in her thoughts, Sarah visited the day of Mark and Lauren's wedding. Now that she and John were moving, there came an excitement in knowing they were beginning a new life. If it were not for the cancer in John's lungs, she could be happy. The doctor thought it was in remission by the test run as scheduled through the year. When she'd told Mark they were leaving the farm he was puzzled.

"But Dad loves the farm. What will you do, sell it?"

"No, Julie and Blaine will farm the land and live in the house."

"Where will you go?"

"Your Dad wants to live in the hills, raise a few cattle."

"Arkansas?"

Sarah chuckled. "Missouri has hills too, fifty miles from here. It's a small farm, mostly valley and pasture with a small creek running through it."

"Imagine that. Dad never sits still."

"The doctor wants him to learn to."

"What will you raise?"

"Roses." They grinned, Mark's eyes lighting up.

"I'll bring you a couple, when we come to visit."

Her heart quickened. Once he'd said when he left, he'd not return. She glanced at him expectantly.

"Now, Mom, I can't come home too often with a new job."

In the following days, Sarah remembered and recognized a moment of pain in Mark's eyes, as he asked, "What about Grandma?"

Moving began the first week of November. Harvest almost complete, John considered weather could move in on them. Myrtle eyed their moving day with a forlorn knowledge she was being left behind.

"You'll have me, Grandma," Julie stated mischievously. "Not that I ever was much important to you but who knows, with the others gone, you may even like me."

"Pshaw." Myrtle spat juice on the grass beyond the side walk. "You underestimate yourself. I always knew where I stood with you. Who do you think you fooled?"

"Really, Grandma?" Julie turned a serious expression on Myrtle. "Let's be friends. I'll miss mom as much as you're going to miss Dad."

"Are you implying I won't miss your Mother?"

Busy packing dishes, Julie grinned. "Well, will you?"

Myrtle snorted. "I've never lived very far from Sarah. Yes, I'll miss her."

"You can baby sit our little girl." Julie cupped her arms around her grandmother. She'd seen her distress.

"I thought there was a catch." Myrtle felt a foolish tug of love around her heart at that moment.

"And we can ride up together to see them." Leaning in Julie whispered. "I worry about Mom."

To his surprise, Mark loved the hill farm and did not stay away. He and Lauren visited often. Walking the hills with his father, helping mend fences, brought them to a new understanding which overshadowed the older man's continued gruffness.

Lauren and Sarah drove into town, browsing the shops, to return home to cook the meal together. Julie thought, sometimes with a tinge of envy, the two were more compatible than in-laws should be but she soothed her conscience, that's what her mother needed, just as she accepted the fact, she and her grandmother had maintained a peace of sorts after years of dissension.

On one occasion as they were driving to visit, Julie said, "I remember when you wouldn't even let me tell Mark stories."

"I know, Julie, girl." Myrtle sighed. "You were so caught up in fairy tales, I feared for you. Never could get you to memorize scripture, so I finally gave up."

"Mark learned enough for both of us, but secretly I retained enough to get me through the hard times."

"You've done well. And you've made a nice home for your family. Your daddy's house doesn't look the same, it's like you, young and fresh and that's not at all disturbing. You got your own way, child."

Patting her rounded stomach, Julie sighed. "It won't be just me and Blaine before long. We'll have our little girl."

For the most part, they were counterparts but there were days Julie in the last stage of pregnancy would declare at the breakfast table, "I'm not calling her. She got on my case about doing things on time and I don't like it. I'm not calling."

Blaine sputtered in his coffee cup. "You know you will. The problem may be," he'd tilt his head studying her with fondness; "the two of you are too much alike."

"We certainly are not."

"You know what they say, take a busy bossy child and you'll probably have a busy, bossy adult."

"I never heard that. You just made that up."

"Well, I like the old girl. She's got spunk and I just imagine if I looked down the road into the future, I'll see you. She may be bossy but you thrive on it and if it weren't for her we couldn't get half as much done around here." He rose to leave. "I know you are trying to impress her."

"Out." She pointed to the door as he buzzed a kiss on her cheek. Unwanted the grin came. Hers.

Then, Lissie entered the world, claiming Grandma's heart; a little girl for whom she would make dresses with rows of tucks and lace edging, using all those fine skills the tailor had taught her as a girl. Sarah Elizabeth was on her birth certificate but it was Grandma said, "Hello little Lissie. We're going to be best friends."

The seasons continued on in their age old pattern and Blaine and Julie were broke in to the patterns of parenting. By the time spring planting arrived, they were sleep deprived; with Blaine wondering how he would stay awake to plant corn. It was late March and Julie decided to forego planting potatoes. She was that tired. Who said parenthood was easy she wondered as she settled into the rocker, Lissie staring up with solemn eyes now that it was daylight when in the night she awakened with a cooing sound ready to be held.

"Got her days and nights mixed," Grandma would say. "You think your folks will drive down today?"

She's got some sixth sense, Julie thought, she seems to know when they're coming. How will I ever get a meal prepared with this baby in my arms? But she didn't have too. Sarah brought a basket full of food and leftovers for the next day. It was her guilt offering for not being there for Julie. On the other hand, John was mesmerized with Lissie, talking to her in a melodic voice, singing an Irish tune Julie supposed he'd sang to her.

"Remember the cotton choppers, Dad?" Swing Low, he'd hum until the song bubbled up, wanting out and Lissie would listen, her head against his chest hearing the thrumming of his heart.

"It sure is hard to leave you, little girl," he'd whisper in Lissie's ear upon leaving and Julie knew the words were for her, too.

"Ga-mama coming today?" The months passed quickly, one seemingly like the other as Julie watched her little girl grow and now she was forming sentences; standing at the window, on tiptoe, trying to see down the road, watching for the big yellow school bus that brought Grandma. An old friend of the family was the driver and he invited Myrtle Buchanan to ride out mornings and back in of the evenings. Beginning his route, she would be the first off and the last picked up, it worked out fine.

"Not today, Lissie, maybe tomorrow." Julie sighed. "It should've been Mark living here." She thought of her brother every day. Lissie giggled hearing his name. She liked Uncle Mark. "But he didn't want to farm," Julie continued, pouting. "But I think he's happy with Aunt Lauren." A smile tugged at her as she pulled herself together mentally for another day and made her body rise up out of the chair. "I'm happy with your daddy but I'm tired. Farming is not for the faint of heart. I think I'm just that, today."

Another crop year completed. Mark and Lauren were in for the weekend. The family was celebrating Lissie's third birthday. The birthday cake put her to sleep while the family sat talking about the war.

"It has developed slowly for the United States involvement," John said. "But the news reports our forces in Vietnam have grown from twenty three thousand in Nineteen Sixty One, to one hundred eighty thousand in sixty five. I heard one reporter say the number would double by the end of the year. "He sighed, wearily."

"That's over a half million," Blaine whistled. "How did it all get started anyway?"

Julie knew her dad always listened to the news and he had a good mind for figures. "I don't understand any of it, Dad, but you tried to explain it to me once, didn't you?"

"It goes back to the fifties." John shook his head, solemnly. "When President Truman gave aid to the French in their war against the Vietnamese. Then Eisenhower gave even more material support to their government and that passed on down through Kennedy and Johnson."

"What do you think it's about, Dad?" Mark asked.

"Who knows? Johnson says it's to stop aggression and preserve the freedom of the South Vietnamese. I'm afraid our politicians do double talk sometimes. You have to remember in sixty six Johnson's administration supported General Thieu when he seized control of the same government."

"We never know what's going on, do we?"

"Probably not, but this election race will bring out the leaks, it always does. Already they're saying the tonnage of bombs being dropped there exceeds that of Europe during World War Two."

"Those were serious times, it's where John's brother's fought," Sarah explained.

"It's serious for us, too, isn't it?" Marks asked, quietly. He waited for his father's reply.

"It seems to me it's been getting more serious over the Tonkin Gulf episode."

"Yeah, I hear the men talk about that." Blaine nodded.

"Our government," John said, "Says they were attacked while patrolling that area in International waters, by North Vietnamese torpedo boats, but our own Senator Fulbright questions whether that's true."

"I don't understand why our government would lie about something like that?" Mark said.

"From what the news releases give account," John replied, "Our intervention seems to be bringing together the Communist super powers." For a moment John considered the information his brothers often supplied from their own experience in war zones. "To escalate the war, Blaine."

"It's a mess," Blaine agreed. "You spend more time trying to decipher what they really mean than understanding any of it."

"Exactly. Are we aiding and abetting or preventing Communist control?"

It was as if everyone walked on egg shells, careful lest they borrow trouble. They could feel Mark thinking. His high school buddies were signing into branches of service. They didn't want him to think he had to rush into a decision based on his friends. It was a time when some were drafted and others joined by choice. Then the news reports stated the war was escalating.

Christmas season brought a frenzied rush to buy gifts. "We need to make this one special, don't we, Mom?"

"That tells me either you know something or feel it; it's about Mark joining up, isn't it?"

"When can we put up your tree?"

"You are side-stepping the issue, aren't you." Sarah's hand was on Julie's arm. "Tell me."

"I think he will, Mom. He's that kind of man." She squeezed her mother's hand. "So let's make it good." Pulling into a parking place, she studied her mother. Sadness was written on her face. "Mom, we have to get our shopping done today. I have to hurry home afterwards and Mark and Lauren will be here tomorrow. You have to get your list out and get the shopping finished. Yes?"

Sarah nodded but her heart was not into shopping. How did parents smile and send their child off to war?

Mark and Lauren arrived, the back seat of the car loaded with gifts. Carrying them in, Lauren placed a red fur clad Santa on the dining room table. "Merry Christmas, Mrs. Buchanan, this should keep you smiling." She pressed a small lever and the figure became animated; Santa was swinging his arms, moving his knees and laughing a jolly ho ho ho. Sarah's laughter was all Lauren needed as she hugged her mother in law. "He's cute, isn't he?"

"Come on in." Sarah motioned to the living room. "What do you think? Julie was here yesterday and helped me move the furniture for the Christmas tree. I figure Mark will want to find one on the hill but if he doesn't I have that silver one in the basement."

Chapter Nine

Mark thought the logical thing to do would be to join, in order to have a choice in which branch of the armed services he would serve. He chose the Air Force. As time for leaving drew near, Mark and Lauren stayed with their parents in order to have more time with them and to relieve Lauren the burden of moving their possessions by herself.

To Sarah, there was a quietness in the two as they would steal away to walk down by the creek with its bubbling waters or climb the hill holding hands and stop often to cling to each other. Mark had finished training in Biloxi, Mississippi, gone on to Florida for further training and returned to Missouri resigned to their future. For Lauren, Sarah knew it was bittersweet, these last days together and she prayed that neither Lauren nor she would break under the circumstance of Mark's absence.

Mark made a special trip down to see Bill. Bill worked for Blaine now, and it was time to tell Bill and Letty and Joe Lynn goodbye.

"You come back home safe," Bill said, pumping Mark's hand to finally throw his arms around this boy he'd helped raise.

"I'll probably meet you over there," Joe Lynn said, grinning. "I think I'd like a little of the excitement."

"This will be hard on your Momma." Letty was crying. "I wish you weren't going."

"It will be hard on the great John Buchanan." Joe Lynn added. He gave Mark a slap on the back.

"Don't be disrespectful, son," Bill admonished.

Mark drove away, Letty crying and her words bouncing around in his head. "Oh, Mark, how can your Momma stand it?" But there was another problem. Lauren found out she was pregnant and if they understood clearly, Lauren overheard a whispered discussion between Blaine and Julie and she thought Julie was pregnant, too. He was leaving Lauren at a time when she needed him. She could not accompany him over seas. Now the remaining days pressed heavily on the family, Mark most of all. He sat playing his mother's organ, hour after hour, sometimes the notes wailing their sad song.

Julie was with her mother, walking in the garden as the sound wafted through an open window. "How do you bear that?"

"It's when I no longer hear it, that I think I can't bear it," Sarah replied quietly.

"You are so brave, Mom." Julie reached for her mother's hand "How is Dad handling everything?"

Sarah's shoulders heaved, "It's eating him up." She swallowed down the grief she wished to wallow in. "He talked to your brother last night."

"What did he say?" Trepidation claimed Julie for a moment. But surely Dad wouldn't hurt Mark, now.

Seeing Julie's expression, Sarah hurried to reply. "He told him how proud he is of him, and how sorry all the years past, they pulled apart with neither understanding why?" Tears glistened in Sarah's eyes. She tried to blink them away, staring to where sunlight rimmed clouds above the hill. "Mostly, they wrapped their arms around each other and cried. We all cried."

"Oh, Mom, it's all so heavy. But I'm glad they talked. It was Daddy saying good bye, wasn't it?"

"I suppose." Sarah wiped her eyes. "We have cried so many times, I'm ashamed to say it. Maybe I'm like my mother, she cried when people gave her a card."

"Maybe," Julie replied, gently. "These are times when families all around us are hurting. When families love each other, they cry. It's all right, Mom."

"I try to hide my tears, Julie, truly I do."

Mark stood proudly before them in service dress. He looked too young to be going away. Julie thought of the length of time, not seeing him and she clutched Blaine's hand wondering how Lauren would handle the separation. Lissie's little face wore an expression of admiration. Who knew what a child understood? It was Grandma whose gaze seemed to look beyond the occasion, her spare form trembling as she raised her face as Mark came to her, now.

"Goodbye, Grandma, I'll miss you." Crushing that frail body to his own, he remembered all the hours he'd sit on her knee, reading, while she listened, adding a word when needed, encouraging him on. "You are the best. I'll miss you. Now don't do anything to hurt your health." He grinned. "None of that gardening in the rain and no walking out to Julie's."

"Pshaw, you know I can't do that anymore." She was pleased when he hugged her again, seeming unable to let go. "I love you," they said together and there was a sprinkling of tears they tried to hide.

Mark gripped Blaine's hand, there was a slap on the back as the two stared long and hard at each other, until the bear hug come with Blaine saying, "I don't want to mess up your uniform." Then Mark moved on to Julie.

He hugged her so tight she thought he'd crack a few bones. "Who's going to watch out for me, Julie?" He whispered. "You've done it all these years, but over there I'll be alone."

"I'll be praying for you, Mark. We all will. There's things I want to say, but I'll write them to you."

"That's what I'll need, Julie. I'm counting on you." Mark heard the engine start up on the airplane.

He turned to his father. He'd dreaded this moment from the time he'd signed up. Looking into his father's eyes, all the years passed between them. And the sweet release when they'd tried harder.

"Take it easy, Dad." John Buchanan's strong form began to tremble as his knees buckled against his son and Mark's arms went around his father. They all heard John's agonizing cry, as the airplane's revving sound turned quieter, a door opened and portable steps were aligned to its side. John turned away from the group as Mark tucked his head on his mother's shoulders and whispered in her ear.

Sarah held his head between each hand, looking into his face to kiss each cheek. "I'm proud of you, Mark; don't ever forget how much we love you. I love you." Carry that with you her words were saying.

Now Mark's heart beat until he thought it would leap out of his chest as he folded Lauren to his body. The fury in his mind was like nothing he'd known. What were they facing? Would Lauren be all right? Frenzied, the thoughts came then vanished as the pilot increased power to the engine. He pressed Lauren close, to remember in the months ahead, while she whispered, "Don't leave me, Mark."

Julie couldn't stand it. She went to stand by her father. Lauren's low moans reminded her of a funeral cry, whimpering at first to rise in agony, filled with pain as the hurt of an innocent child.

She heard Lauren's whispered farewell. "I love you, Mark."

She knew their hearts cried out, as one, silently willing him to return home, safe.

They watched Mark climb the steps to the plane and waited until he was seated by the window. There was stiffness in his shoulders as he stared out seeing nothing but gray mist between him and his family. His lips tightened lest a moan of despair escape. He wasn't brave, the turmoil reared up to claim him. Sweat broke out on his brow. He'd joined to keep from being called, thinking it was his duty and he wanted to do what was right, but it wasn't fair to leave one's family for some war-torn land that pledged allegiance under a different flag. And then there they were, his family, huddled together, waving, while Lauren clung to his mother. His father half- turned away, as though his body was doing battle with his mind and Mark understood.

His life was in the hands of others. He would do what they said. Something inside gripped him, as he heard the door close and saw the steps rolled away. His eyes were on Lauren. *I'll be back. I'll be back. Do you hear me? Trust in the Lord what time you're afraid. I'll be back.* The flight was a blur, changeover a must, automatically performed. The picture of Lauren beckoned to him as she stood on the hillside, blonde hair blowing in the wind.

Arriving in Korea, for special training before his intended destination, Vietnam, Mark's world became a people of dark eyes, olive skin unlike his mother's with a yellowish tint. Straight hair, bowing and shuffling they farmed their soil much as their ancestors, with crude tools. He'd made a few friends. They all seemed boyishly young. One, Alex Greenly from Mississippi, said, "You know I keep thinkin' of my Momma at home and fried chicken and apple pie" He grinned, foolishly as his large body tilted toward Mark. "Ain't that somethin' to keep one's mind busy?"

During 1968 it was rumored the Viet Cong struck in almost every city of Vietnam. The Tet Offensive launched by the North Vietnamese and Viet Cong was the most fierce and cruel attacks as they entered the towns of the people. It was their attempt to create rebellion in the people and an effort to encourage the United States to disengage from the war. Their victory would be known if the U.S. withdrew from that region. While fruitless negotiations began between the United States and North Vietnamese governments, Mark's family worried increasingly as they received the news.

Julie received a letter from her brother in September. "I miss everyone," he said, "but I worry about Lauren. The other night I dreamed we were back in Biloxi where I took my training. We loved it there. All at once I awoke and realized I wasn't there. It doesn't seem fair to be away from Lauren while we are expecting the baby."

In the two months since Mark's leaving, the crops were turning toward harvest. Julie with Lissie's hand in hers walked to the farm shop to deliver a message. Letty passed by, honking and waving, seeing Bill on the shop yard, she slowed and then sped on.

"Where's Letty headed?"

"She's going to town to buy Joe Lynn new clothes. He's taking a job in the city since the Marines won't have him."

"Why's that? I haven't seen Joe Lynn or Letty in a while. Why won't they have him?"

"Blaine didn't tell you?" Bill glanced up from where he was tightening nuts on a wheel. "He has a heart murmur."

"A heart murmur?" Julie's face registered remorse. "I'm sorry."

"Yep, they asked him if he'd ever had a sore throat. There was that time when he was a kid, the doctor warned us he could develop Rheumatic Fever and maybe he did because that's what they're thinking caused the heart murmur."

"Are you and Letty driving him up?"

"No, he had it all figured out, talked me and his ma into going along with his idea. I resisted long as I could until he says if you don't help me, I'll find a way to buy it myself."

"A car." Julie nodded. "He'll need something."

"No, he got a motorcycle. A big one." Pulling himself up from the squatting position, Bill's mouth set in a straight line as he was thinking. "Dangerous, is what they are and him with a bit of a wild streak."

"He'll grown up, Bill. Mark did."

"Mark was never wild like our boy, Julie." Bill's word, said gentle were not a rebuke." How is Mark?"

"I guess you heard, Lauren's expecting a baby after first of the year. They're both terribly lonely."

They were in harvest before they knew it. Julie waited on the end of the turn row for Bill to dump beans on the grain truck. It was a late Friday afternoon. Whereas the sky had been clear and a sun shine that sparkled on the land, the clouds now bore sign of rain. Scanning the horizon, Julie saw puffs of dust now and then on the field road until a helmeted rider drew nearer on a motorcycle.

Bill pulled the release lever on the auger of the combine, emptied the holding tank of beans and shut down the combine as he stepped out onto the platform. He groaned recognizing the rider.

"Hey, Pop," Joe Lynn called up to him. "Come on down, examine these wheels." When Bill hesitated, he grabbed the rail to swing himself up. "Ain't they something?"

The inspection took less than five minutes. Discouraged, Bill climbed back up the ladder to the cab.

"I don't think Pop's none too pleased with my wheels, do you?"

"He's just afraid you'll be hurt out in city traffic. Did you have any trouble coming home?"

"No, I didn't. Everything's working the way its suppose to." Joe Lynn's eyes followed as Bill turned the combine down the rows. "Have you priced a car lately, Julie? Well, I did and they are quite pricey. I'll save a heap of money on gas with this thing."

"It's the city traffic, Joe Lynn, try not to take chances."

"Who me?" Joe Lynn laughed. "The city is a piece of cake, in and out of traffic. A breeze."

The months passed with Mark's letters trickling through their lives, an absence felt as the holidays arrived and Joe Lynn arrived to celebrate Christmas with his folks, stopping in to inquire about Mark.

"Man," he exclaimed, "Me and Mark killed a lot of Indians out there in that ole' chicken yard." His statement brought laughter and reminder of the two who thought they were invincible riding stick horses with toy guns on their hips shooting imaginary things which in reality were just chickens.

Sarah baked the usual festive pies and cakes but when serving time came, she couldn't eat Mark's favorite. "Neither can I," Julie and Lauren stated, together, laughing as the ache in their heart eased.

"What's wrong with this pie, if you won't eat it?" John demanded. Suddenly everyone was quiet; their eyes staring across space to where Mark's picture in uniform sat on the buffet. John followed their gaze. "I see." He pushed his plate away. "Why'd you make Mark's favorite if none of us feel like eating it?"

"It's Christmas."

A wave of sadness hit his chest. "Yes, it is." His eyes lift to meet Sarah's, their pain bared to all. "But we have each other and we must go on until Mark returns." He was silent thinking of years past, bitter years…but there were others. "When he was little, our little blue eyed boy wanted a tractor. It was more than we could afford but we heard of this factory you could order from, that the items were half price if you assembled them yourself. We did just that and it took us all night to assemble that thing." Remembering, a smile play about John's lips as his eyes brightened. "We wished we'd paid the price."

"I don't remember Mark liking tractors that much," Julie remarked. "He liked the team of mules, though. I'm surprised if he didn't particularly like tractors that you'd buy one for him."

"That's the reason we did." Gruffness came into his voice. "Christmas is for children."

"Christmas," Myrtle Buchanan said, "Is to celebrate a baby born in a manager who would lay down his life for us that we might live through eternity. It's for children, that's true, but for us, also. There's the real reason. A heavenly father who would send His son to die for our sins. That's Christmas."

Chapter Ten

Mark and Lauren's son was born red as a rose screaming his lungs out on a crisp January morning in 1969 while drops of snow spit through the air. While visiting the hospital Julie stared out the window thinking of her brother's last letter. "They strap bombs on their children and send them into our midst. What a world to bring a child into. And they fatten the dogs to eat for meat. It's a different world, sis. Sometimes I can't believe I'm here."

Leaving the hospital Lauren bided time between little Brent's grandparents homes. At the end of February Julie received a letter from Mark, saying, "Sis, by the time I see Brent he will be eight months old, if they let me come home then. It doesn't seem possible, my being a daddy. I guess because I'm not there. I cry, Sis, because I'm not there. Julie, wouldn't dad be disappointed to know I cried? Remember how he used to whip me and I wouldn't cry? Lord, Julie, I wish I could see everyone. Dad and Mom are getting older. Did I ever tell dad, enough, that I loved him? I love you sis."

We went on recce today. Reconnaissance gives me the creeps. It's because we don't know what will happen. I mean it gives me the willies. This land is like shadows, you can't see what's out there. You can tell I'm feeling a little low. Everyone here is in the same boat. Write me, Julie. I'm a little tense. I need to hear. I love you. Your brother, Mark.

Julie lay her head on the kitchen table and cried. No, Mark, Daddy wouldn't be disappointed at all. He cries a lot. It's as if someone knocked the breath out of him and Mom is just a shadow slipping in and out of rooms.

Myrtle called each day, the first words betraying her attempt to hide loneliness. But it lightened her spirit knowing Julie was coming for her to spend the day. And joy returned to her heart knowing there was still someone who loved her when it seemed everyone had gone away.

Mark and Lauren had hoped Mark could return for a visit when their son was born. A military hop could cost as little as ten dollars if an enlisted person saved up leave time but Mark would be at the mercy of hitch-hiking once he reached the states. The family discussed the possibilities, if they knew when he was to arrive, someone would be there. Then he'd written Lauren, saying it was not possible. *"I've received orders, they're sending me to Vietnam. If this last conflict had not developed, it's ironic; they are sending home a bunch of convicts. Can you imagine? Our own men."*

Myrtle and Julie were drawn into a strange alliance. It was as if everyone was holding their breath waiting for the war to end. Instead they heard remarks, such as, "The Young boy's funeral is today." Through pressed lips, Myrtle would say, "I knew that family. God rest their souls."

Julie had another birthday. "I remember my earlier birthdays by chores," she laughed. "I progressed from carrying a pot in the days before inside toilets in our bathroom and I hated that job, then I carried coal buckets too large for my strength but Momma would say don't load them so heavy. Then there was cotton chopping, as a half-hand and cotton picking began with a little sack that seemed to grow longer as the years passed for me and Mark. "Isn't that a strange way to remember your life?"

Blaine hugged her tightly to his body. He realized the closeness between Julie and Mark hid a million secrets that had nothing to do with their lives presently. He understood there had been problems between Mark and his father even before he came on the scene and in the beginning Julie had a reluctance to share the discord, fearing he would not like her father and judge him unfairly. "Dad's a good man, Blaine. I just can't explain to you these things happened in our family and it's not easy to talk about."

"I know, honey, I'm in the family now. You don't have to be ashamed.

We're all a bit dysfunctional."

"But why do I worry over Mark?"

"Turn it loose, Julie. Mark's a man. He may have scars from the past but he'll be a better man because of it. He's got Lauren and the new baby. Let it go."

Julie began to notice signs of weakness in her grandmother. She couldn't put a finger on what was happening, but Grandma's usual love of gardening was abandoned. There were no flowers in the huge pots by the door and she was beginning to say she'd not ride along when Julie visited her parents in the hills.

"I don't know what's going on with grandma." She waited for her mother to meet her gaze. "Do you?"

Sarah stopped ironing, standing the iron upright on the metal guard. "Has she been to the doctor?"

"She wouldn't let me take her. I did ask but she said there's nothing wrong here I can't handle."

"We'll be down, tomorrow but don't let her know we're coming."

They came as Sarah promised, although she confided at first John had been reluctant. "I told him, this is your mother. I'm going. Stay if you wish." Sarah's gray eyes lit up for a moment. "You see him, don't you?"

"Lissie is staying with Blaine, when we go to see Grandma. I'm ready when you and Dad say we can go."

Surprised, still wearing her night gown and wrapper, Myrtle met them at the door. Her beautiful white hair lay on her shoulders, not in its usual round on top of her head with the pearl combs on the sides. "You didn't call," her eyes narrowed as she glanced Julie's way. "Have you been up to mischief, girl?"

"Why, Mrs. Buchanan." Sarah feigned a laugh. "We thought to surprise you. I brought lunch."

"That you did, surprise me, I mean." Myrtle was twisting her hair, drawing the plastic pins from the wrapper pocket to deftly secure it on top of her head. "Just let me get dressed. Go sit down, in there." She almost carried off her independence, when a pain hit that staggered her walk and released a gasp.

Sarah being nearest rushed to place a hand beneath Myrtle's arm, steadying her. "Is the pain bad?" She asked as though they discussed the pain every day. "I'm going to help you dress, and then we'll talk."

"Sarah," Myrtle's voice was fretful. "I don't want to bother anyone, nor be a burden to you or John."

"We've neglected you, Mrs. Buchanan, allowing you that stubborn independence your family deems important. We're done with that. Tomorrow I'm going with you to see a different doctor. That's final."

Tears gathered in Myrtle's eyes. Hadn't she prayed to the Lord for help? And he'd sent Sarah.

It wasn't good. The doctor's eyes met Sarah's as he examined Mrs. Buchanan. "Is there anything you might tell me to shed light on why this woman hasn't come to see me before now?"

"Her doctor told her it's a hernia and she could bind it to keep the pain bearable, except now it isn't."

"We'll run a few tests with you staying overnight, Mrs. Buchanan. Now don't protest. We have to."

Heartbroken, Julie received the news, telling Blaine. "Grandma has cancer." Turning into his arms, she asked, "How can I deal with this, Blaine? And Daddy says I'm not to tell Mark. He told Lauren the same. He thinks we could cause Mark to lose focus and right now Mark can't tell us what he's doing. Dad thinks it's dangerous."

"Your Dad is taking a big responsibility, Julie. He's making a decision I wouldn't want, myself."

She visited Grandma in the hospital. On that day there were tubes running from her stomach and Myrtle Buchanan was in much pain. When the pain was at its utmost, Myrtle tried to pull the tubes from her stomach. When the medicine relieved the pain to bearable, she begged Julie to loosen the restraints the nurse had applied to her wrist to keep her from removing the tubes while she was delirious.

When the nurses worked with her grandmother, Julie hid out in the bathroom, crying her heart out. Later she would wail, "I can't stand it Blaine. She's suffering. What has she done to deserve this?"

After a week's stay, the doctor put Myrtle Buchannan on morphine and allowed John and Sarah to take her to their home. "I'm sending a nurse out to teach you how to administer the drugs," he told Sarah. "There's nothing more can be done but keep your mother in law comfortable."

When the pain was at bay, Sarah and Julie talked with Myrtle on whatever subject seemed dear to her at the moment. "When are you expecting the baby?" Myrtle asked Julie.

"How do you know? I haven't told anyone. Except, Blaine."

"You're too worried about me, aren't you, Julie girl?" Myrtle's hand sought Julie's. "Julie, I wanted to see your new baby and see Mark come home but we all know none of that's going to happen." Myrtle sighed. "I love you, Julie, always have but I wanted to curb that impulsive nature you seemed bent on at times and I can see my job is finished." She produced the hint of a smile. "I mean that kindly, Julie. You're a beautiful young woman, inside out and I know Blaine treasures who you are."

"Grandma." Julie lay her head on the side of the bed and sobbed. "I can't lose you, Grandma." Her nose was running snot, and her grandmother produced a clean handkerchief, handing it to her.

"Blow your nose, girl," she said, just as she did when Julie was a child. "Now you got a lot to think about with Blaine and Lissie and the farm work. So you stay healthy because this new little boy is going to add to your work. But he's going to bless your life, Julie girl, just like Lissie has."

"A boy, Grandma? Are you sure?"

In the next three months, anyone observing would have thought Myrtle Buchanan was Sarah's mother. Sarah cooked and pureed foods that Mrs. Buchanan could eat, noticing the amount became smaller as her body shrunk beneath the sheet, the indention of her boniness prodded Sarah to try more foods, finally to offer her mother in law baby food with bland seasoning in hopes it would digest.

"Let her die with dignity," the cancer doctor encouraged. "She does not want feeding tubes and use of them would only prolong her demise."

"She is a person, doctor, not a study and I want to do the best I can for her."

In his profession, he was trained for the animosity that often arose between the patient's relatives and the honor of the medical staff, concerning their loved one. "I realize your pain. We are telling you what is best for your mother and our patient, if that does not meet your…"

"She is not my mother, sir, but I would treat any person with regard when they lay suffering."

"You are to be commended," he replied gently. "But if she eats then there's the question what the body has to do with consumption. Do you understand? There's an old rule, what goes in must go out."

Sarah flushed, embarrassed that she had questioned his skill and knowledge. "Yes." She understood.

From that point on, when Myrtle said, "Sarah, the thought of food makes me ill. Thank you for all you do for me, but I don't believe I need more than a thimble full each meal," Sarah removed the item. Julie listened, thinking there had always been a bond between the two.

Julie felt the tiredness of the fifty mile trip, but she also felt compelled to go; taking Myrtle's hand in her own, tracing the length of their fingers, more the same than hers and her mother's. She brushed her grandmother's hair, placed the pearl combs just so, that they would not push into her scalp as she lay on the pillow and then one day she was reluctant to leave, a great foreboding pressing around her heart.

"But there's Lissie," her grandmother reminded her through parched lips.

"No, Grandma, Lissie is with me, today. Momma has her in the kitchen." "I forgot, "she whispered. "Julie, girl, she is too little to watch me die."

Julie kissed her brow, tasting the saltiness of sweat, wondering at the coolness of her skin. "Are you warm, Grandma?"

"No, Julie, I'm cold. My feet feel numb and I can hardly tell they're there."

Myrtle Buchannan died in her son's home with those she loved and who loved her, all present except Mark. She accepted Sarah's explanation that Mark could not come home, turning her face to the wall to prevent anyone seeing her tears.

"My body is so tired, Julie," she whispered through parched lips. "Tell me you will be all right when you go through life without me hounding you." She heard the sob as Julie came to her bedside. "Tell Mark I miss him but I'll be watching for him one day when he's done with this world…and your daddy, Julie, you must watch over him. Whether he knows it or not, he is going to miss me." She tried to smile but a cough strangled her, leaving her spent. Two days later she died quietly, the horror of the last month's pain left behind with Julie curled into a fetal position at her feet, one hand protectively on her stomach.

"We could buy a dress," Sarah paused. "What do you think, Julie?"

"I think Grandma would want to be buried in the dress she wore to Mark and Lauren's wedding."

Chapter Eleven

Mark clutched the piece of paper in his hand, clenched his eyes tightly shut and leaned against the tree. He felt its rough bark but he didn't care. For a second he pondered the name of the tree, wondering why? Maybe it was an oak. Miles from home, only a few trees and he didn't know this one's name. Why was he considering a tree? The captain had called him into his office, spoken the few necessary words and handed him the paper.

His buddy came out of the barracks, laughing. A scurry of feet behind him meant someone was after him. There was the sound of bodies scuffling and voices loud and boisterous threatening retaliation. "I'll get you, Blue, you too, Henderson."

Jim Blue stopped short, seeing the expression on Mark's face. "Is something wrong, Mark?"

Mark shook his head, waving him on, watching as he stuffed his winnings in his pocket. He'd tried to teach Mark different card games but Mark's heart wasn't in it. "Just don't get in any important games," Jim Blue declared. "They'd skunk you for sure. What do you like Mark? Surely there's something."

Mark knew what had come easy to him was learning scripture, encouraged by Grandma.

He was a man in a stupor. Grandma gone? He couldn't believe they waited until last minute to tell him. Lauren had gone against his father's wishes, allowing it to be told. The captain received her call while Mark was out, on reconnaissance, dropped down by a helicopter crew into the dense forest to spy on Charlie; while they forgot he was there and continued spraying Agent Orange on the foliage.

Barracks were empty. His unit had been granted some rare downtime. The guys would go into town to find girls, drink themselves into a stupor and spend the next day reviving before going back on active duty. He sank onto the bed, swung his booted feet up onto the blanket and lay there stretched full length and rigid. Weekends didn't exist, each day was just another day at war. Deployed airmen and soldiers might get furlough or be taken off line a few days but weekends were for state side troops not at war. But how was he going to get through the hours alone, with no one there to grieve with him?

Let not your heart be troubled. Ye believe in God, believe also in me. In my father's house are many mansions, if it were not so, I would have told you. I go to prepare a place for you. And if I go and prepare a place for you, I will come again and receive you unto myself; that where I am, there ye may be also. And whither I go, ye know, and the way ye know.

Yea, though I walk through the valley of the shadow of death, I will fear no evil; for thou art with me; they rod and thy staff they comfort me. Thou preparest a table before me in the presence of mine enemies; thou anointest my head with oil; my cup runneth over. Surely goodness and mercy shall follow me all the days of my life and I will dwell in the house of the Lord, forever. Amen.

"Hey, buddy? Mark?" It was Jim Blue. "What're you layin' in the dark, for, Mark?" He sank onto the opposite bed. "They wouldn't let me go with them since I won most of their money. Say, what's wrong?" Mark handed the paper to Jim, turning his body; his face to the wall.

For a change John and Sarah drove down to the farm. Julie was beginning to form a bump with her pregnancy and this time her feet swelled. That concerned Sarah. Thus, they arrived, Sarah carrying a hamper full of food, Lauren following behind with Brent in her arms. "Oh," Julie, cooed mesmerized by her nephew's growth and the glow on Lauren's face.

"Did you hear from Mark this week?"

"No." Julie motioned they should sit. Settling in she asked, "Is there something special I need to know?" She accepted the letter Lauren offered. "Here, read mine."

"You sure?"

"Well, I left off the last page, didn't figure you'd be interested in that one."

Julie nodded. She was already reading. *Dear Lauren, I received your letter about Grandma. I've read it over and over. It doesn't seem possible that she's gone and I won't see her when I return. At least I find comfort in knowing she loved me. And there was never any doubt how much I loved her. I don't blame you for not letting me know until last minute but it did take me awhile to understand dad's reasoning. He should have let them inform me. I might have been able to come home but it would have changed the length of time I'd have to stay here when I returned. Maybe seeing someone you love helps to realize they are really gone. My buddy says it brings closure. But he says a lot of things. I don't know. I still see Grandma in that funny little garden behind her house. It hurts being away. Sometimes I'm ashamed how it hurts because you'd think I was stronger by now but I'm not. I miss the family. I've been down in spirit the last few weeks, I guess with Grandma dying and my longing to see you and our son. It makes me realize how easily something could happen to one of us. I say Brent's name over and over and I look at the picture of you and him. Are you doing all right? Is the old station wagon running good enough? I worry over you. You know Grandma never mentioned how sick she was but sometimes her handwriting was so shaky I could barely read it. I expected to see her when I come back to the states and tell her all the things brought to mind I thought she'd want to hear about. I miss you so terribly. I think missing you takes my mind off of what I'm doing here. Weekends are the hardest when the other guys go into town which I found is no place for me. Some of the married guys go, but I honor you too......*

Laughing, Julie handed back the letter. "I guess that's where it got deep, huh?" She teased. "I never knew he had it in him."

"Stop it. You'd be the same way if Blaine was gone."

"I know and you don't have to share. I realize there's personal things you both must say."

"I don't mind." Tears tinged Lauren's lashes. "It's hard though. Mark hasn't seen his son."

"Does he say what he is doing?"

"Only that they are training him more. In the states he trained in radio. Surely that's what he does."

"Want to read my last letter?" Seeing Lauren's nod, Julie went in to the bedroom to get it. "It's over a month old and a bit crumpled I've read it so many times."

"I know." There was a reverence in Lauren's voice. "Oh, Julie, how long do you think 'til he comes home?" She scanned Julie's letter, where he asked about Lissie and Blaine but most of all about her.

"I miss Lauren and I ache to see our little boy. I've had a time since I got here. The first two weeks you remember we spent in a tent and someone helped themselves to two of my shirts. It rained all the days and nights and I think I got pneumonia. Everyone was sick because our tent leaked. Now, at least I'm at base. The work is good though and pretty interesting. We have soft beds a locker and a dresser a piece and a small bedside table which really surprised me for military provisions. The barrack is about twenty five feet wide and eighty feet long with the shower another fifty feet from the barracks. In the other end there are seven Army guys plus seven higher up Air

Force in the middle and it is always noisy. I know you have to have specific details. I remember your stories and your characters right down to the wart on the toes of their feet. There are times I could use a few of your stories to put me to sleep at night. Seems like these guys all think of their families at night because that's when they start telling about them. There's some pretty funny stuff. It makes me think of everyone and I get a bit blue. And I remember you would always end by saying and they all received the golden promises. These people could use those promises."

"I don't know Lauren," Julie answered."

"When he does, how hard do you think it will be to readjust?"

"He says it's a different culture over there and when he returns he intends to appreciate everything here." Julie saw Lauren's eyes brighten with tears, though she tried to brush them away.

But Julie," Lauren's face turned sad. "He is going to miss seeing your Grandma so much."

Chapter Twelve

Julie remembered Lauren's words the next morning when she reached for the phone, halting as she started to dial. Why, did she forget and start to call Grandma at the beginning of the day? Although Mark's letters were often weeks apart, she found three in the mailbox. Praying they would not make her sad, she settled onto the sofa to read.

Julie, I don't know why the Christian world seems so complacent in contrast to this world of war. The country is beautiful with hills and mountain streams. The homes are dirt and concrete with straw roofs and dirt floors. They seem to be a happy people but when they look at us we feel they are thinking, we are rich lucky G.I.'s. The average man's income over here is one hundred to one hundred fifty dollars a year and they are the hardest workers I've seen. The weather is hot of the day time and cool of the night. And it rains. I don't know if our military mail goes by ship or plane or carrier pigeon but all of our mail is delayed and your letters help me so much. They lift my spirits so don't quit on me. I like my captain. He always carries a picture of his wife and eleven month old son. They are here with him. He showed me a picture of them the other day. That keeps me thinking of Lauren and our son. While the other guys go to the club to drink and dance with the girls, I seem to spend my time thinking about family right here in the barracks. I'm trying to save up money to buy a guitar to have something to do besides think. I love you, sis. Please keep writing and I'll do my best to reply. Mark

Outside the sunshine beckoned. Get out of the shadow, into the light, Grandma used to say. Now, Julie heard as surely as if she were standing beside her. But she couldn't ignore Mark's second letter, nor the third. She was driven to read the letters while her thoughts read between the lines.

Julie, I'm surviving. How was I to know babies don't get their shots all at once? Have you been reading Lauren's letters? Remember, the last page is for her only. I miss her so much and to think I've a son I haven't seen, except in pictures. We are still going on reconnaissance. Some are kind of scary as we watch the countryside changing around us due to the war and we wish it wasn't. I saw a small patch of cotton the other day and it surprised me. They use a cow for the same purpose Blaine would use a tractor. Otherwise it's all hand labor. I saw my first store, over here. They have everything and it's all in one big pile. Physically, I seem to be fine, but when my check went to another guy with my name and I didn't get any mail from any of you, I started losing weight and my uniforms didn't fit. I nearly flipped out. Then Lauren's letter arrived explaining more about Grandma's death and it helped because all I'd had until then was the telegram that depressed me terribly. Please don't tell the folks or Lauren what I've written I don't mean to worry them but it's good to be able to tell you. I can't really believe Grandma is gone. It can happen so easily for the rest of us but even if she was old, I wanted to see her when I come home. I love you, sis. Write me soon. Mark

It was so obvious Mark's mind was still trying to find closure over their Grandma's death but she also realized there were things he wasn't saying and she couldn't know what he faced each day or the torment of his dreams at night. His gentle soul would not set well with killing or seeing people dying. She opened the third letter, wondering if the ache in her heart could stand more pain.

Julie, I've been searching the scripture, trying to find peace over losing Grandma. When I read the telegram I turned on my side and stared at the wall. Blue sat with me awhile but he didn't know what to say. I don't think he has had much church going back ground but he seems to have a good family that loves him. He talks about his mother's apple pie and fried chicken a lot and makes us all hungry. Pray for me, Julie, sometimes I feel so low and there's nothing to be done about it, we all do but the others seem to go get drunk to quit thinking. Sometimes I'm afraid I'll get so low I can't get back up. And I don't want to think like that. There are things I know will never be the same again and it troubles me. Grandma taught me about God. When you know destruction is near there are times you question if God in Heaven is in complete control. I ran every verse I could during my time of questioning and I'd hear Grandma's voice in my head. She always said, God is in control of his universe. He created it and he knows what will happen to it in the end. But over here, men are controlling the lives of others, deciding their fate and I don't know if it's always what it should be. My fate got tangled in with the whole bit and I resent that. It's possible they won't even send this letter out. I don't know but I'm not the only one questions things. Well, sis, I started out intending to keep this light but I just couldn't hack it. Don't worry about me, I'll get better, I'm just not thinking clearly today. I love you, Julie. Write me. Mark

Rethinking what she knew, Julie pondered the unrest in Mark. He mentioned his work when he was stationed in Korea. *I'm a ground radio operator,* he had written earlier. *The captain and I go out on recee missions. It is our job to find a dummy target for the men training to fly combat missions in Vietnam. Since arriving in Vietnam, there was only one mention when he said we guide the pilots in to spray the defoliant. I hate to see this beautiful green country turn brown and I wonder about the people.*

John Buchanan watched the evening news without fail. He had purchased a map of Vietnam and each evening listening to the names where there was activity, he pinpointed that area on the map.

"Do you worry day and night?" Julie asked. She had driven up to check on them.

"How can we not? If Mark trained with the pilots, common sense tells you he's doing the same thing in Vietnam." John glanced across to where Sarah was ironing. "You know Mark met Sam, the next door neighbor and they struck up a friendship. Sam was in the war, once, maybe that's why they write. Sam had a letter from Mark."

"And?"

"Sam says Mark's the guy they drop down in the woods from helicopter to keep an eye out for any signs of the enemy planes and when he sees something he reports back by radio." John paused, staring at the map. "I asked Sam did Mark say that? He never answered. But he says a strike is when the planes go out to hit the target, meaning the enemy, and you know Mark's been there when they spray to kill the dense foliage and since he is trained in radio surveillance he's there when they hit. I worry they'll forget him when he's there."

Julie surprised her father when she didn't scold his concern and said instead, "I understand, Dad."

"You think he's on one of the big bases, John?" Sarah watched him pinning the spots every night on the map.

"Not necessarily. He's Air Force. According to Sam, each branch keeps its men together."

"But Mark mentioned Marines being in one of the barracks; Air Force on one end and Marines on the other."

"I don't know," John replied. "But a bomb is a bomb. Who knows where they will land and I believe in his letters we are seeing Mark's hurt over innocent people dying although he's not putting it in words And our news is a political façade. They show us what they want us to see, the same for telling."

Julie pondered her father's words, a façade. He read everything. He would describe the war that way. She stared to where Mark's pictures normally sit. One was missing. "Where's the other picture?"

"Lauren takes it with her when she visits her parents." Sarah replied.

Julie wondered where he was, that boy who stared out from the frame, a near shaven head, in uniform, stiff and unrelated to the gentle soft spoken brother she remembered.

Life was good for Julie and Blaine. Their son was born, staring solemnly into their faces, wrapped snug in a blanket waiting to leave the hospital to meet his older sister. Lissie was with Sarah as she and John had driven down to spend the day with their granddaughter while Blaine brought Julie home. Their lives were full but as Sarah often said, they were blessed.

The new baby, as Lissie called him, bothered no one, but all the visitors wanted to hold him. "It's no wonder he sleeps without waking such long hours apart," Julie said, yawning. "I'm worn out. Who would have thought that many people are interested in our baby?"

"New baby," Lissie corrected. "It's my turn next, no matter who is here."

Chapter Thirteen

Mark saw the break of light on the V.C. encampment. He had been dropped on the hillside in the early morning hours. By noon, the heat of the day and the realization that he was alone near the V.C. camp had his nerves on edge and the camouflage clothing was wet with sweat. Radioing his findings, he received reply; he was to wait for the return of the Huey and its pilot, knowing his life depended on their getting through unknown to the Viet Cong.

Waiting was difficult, a man's nerves were at war, frenzied in expectation, cold as steel in what he must do. Under the two o'clock sun he watched the FAC, Forward Air Control, plane circle to the North. Suddenly the V.C. camp stirred. "They're onto us," he whispered, scanning the sky for the Huey, praying it hadn't been shot down.

Something in his line of vision moved. He wiped the sweat from his forehead, eyeing the spot more carefully. What he'd thought to be a mound of hay about three feet high off the ground flattened its rounded shape. Mark blinked, not trusting natural vision as he adjusted the lens of the binoculars. His nerves tightened as blood pounded through his veins. They're close. The questions came, who was moving on the mountain. The people of the area had learned, anything moving was thought by V.C. to be the enemy. If it were the people why hadn't they heard the stirring of the helicopter and where was the sound now? Whether it was V.C. or an innocent became the problem.

Barely breathing, his body still, he watched through the binoculars, his arms were growing tired. Then, he saw a baby toddle out into the open, an arm came from the mound of hay to grasp the child but the child moved farther away, the laughter coming to Mark's ears, echoing through the woods. Only fear would bring an adult out into the open and it was happening right in front of his eyes, a mother reaching for her child, a father trying to pull them both back under cover of the hay.

They were in danger. Foolish. Foolish, to be out in the open. They knew the enemy was close but it was their livelihood, the small patch he'd seen beyond the enemy camp, maybe an acre, possibly two, of crop growing green in an area they had cleared and felt regardless of the danger they must tend. He wondered at their ability to confine a child in the hours since he arrived. On that fact, Mark concluded his presence was known. And he knew, if captured, V.C. soldiers would not be kind.

Their skin might be the same color, God may have deemed them countrymen but fate deemed otherwise. They were at war, one side determined to infringe and claim their land and change their way of thinking. Possibly, some were relatives but it would make no difference in this small family's lives.

A child's cry pierced the air, turning to a wail. Uneasily, fearful V.C. were on alert, Mark scoured the area. Something increased in the FAC plane's engines. Doubtless, they were readying for attack. Where was the helicopter supposed to pick him up? In minutes the fighter bombers would come in, thundering, bombs would be dropped. The babies cry mounted in anguish, suppressed as quickly as it happened, muffled, continuing with a hand or a cloth shoved to the child's mouth. The structure of hay disintegrated, straw falling every direction, thin bodied forms were running in haste toward the trees. Once their long black garments were inside he lost track, either they had fallen to the ground or moved deeper inside the foliage. The drone of the planes increased, where they had circled, now they were coming in fast.

God. They're going to leave me here. Mark panicked. On the wind he caught the smell of smoke. Down in the valley the Marines would be burning the remaining hootches. The homes of the Vietnamese would serve no purpose once the people left. He watched through the binoculars as fires sprang up, here and there, a slight distance between the hootches for privacy, close enough for protection. They were a poor people living where they could to tend those tiny little food patches.

There was movement, the family experiencing the same sensation as Mark must decide, with V.C. on one side, the fire climbing the hill, and the planes coming in and they were uncertain if he was friend or foe. The babies wail was accompanied by a woman's anguished cry as she ran toward him, no pre-set course, just running his direction. A sound exploded, a sniper's bullet making a swishing sound followed by a hard thump as she fell to the ground and the babies cry sounded. Painful, piercing and afraid the child continued to cry as Mark left his spot thinking to drag the parent to safety.

Quickly. Quickly. Leaving cover he saw the bullet had passed through the mother, no doubt continuing its path toward him; otherwise he would not have heard it. Mark threw himself forward, grabbed the baby, tried to regain ground, staggered, almost falling to run back to the shelter of the trees. At first the child squirmed, howling and struggling as Mark ran, his small body dangling from Mark's arm. Mark sat the child down. Turning back, closing the distance, he made purchase of the black figured robe, pulling, dragging, hurrying to collapse by the child as he wondered where the third one was, dead by a bullet or running for his life?

Pulling the hood from the wounded one, he looked into the frightened face of a young woman. Near his age, he couldn't tell, but blood was soaking through the material covering the right side of her body. There was little understanding the reason the father brought them to this field of war; he had to know the V.C. were there and yet his reasoning had failed him as he thought they could elude the V.C. There was no way he could know American planes would appear to make further damage to his homeland. Afraid, she stared back. "You're hit in the shoulder," he explained. Thinking to slow the bleeding he brought the sleeve of her garment to the spot. Fear flashed in her eyes at his touch and she cowered.

A shot rang out, a second and a third, hitting the ground a hundred feet to their right. "They're not sure where we are," Mark said. Now the baby was squalling, rising to toddle toward his mother as Mark swiped away the sweat dripping into his eyes, and thought he saw movement in the trees to his left. The V.C., or the baby's father, his mind streamed a thousand thoughts as the Huey arrived, dipping down in the clearing, the pilot motioning furiously for him to hurry. The mother pushed her son toward Mark. He heard one word. *Pleeeze.* She wanted him to take her child?

Half dragging the woman, the baby looped over his arm with the radio equipment, Mark started across the field. Shots were pelting the ground on all sides. He heard the pilot screaming. "Leave 'em."

"No." A shot whizzed past his shoulder.

"Buchanan. I said leave them. They're V.C."

"No, they're not."

The pilot was pulling him in. "I said leave them. Turn loose, Buchanan or dammit all I'll leave you, too." Mark held tight. "You tryin' to be a hero, Buchanan?" Red faced, he hauled them in, swearing. Now the machine was moving, skirting the area where artillery shells were exploding, pointing down briefly to where a smoldering heap of metal lay on the ground. "They got the helicopter but I got our men."

I wasn't supposed to be left out here. Mark lay back against the metal side. *Thank you, God.*

Twenty minutes later the helicopter set down in a clearing and reloaded into a Medivac helicopter. The Pilot looked at Mark with an amused expression. "You brought us a kid, Buchanan. Now what are we going to do with that?" There were others on the Medivac. Mark ignored the Pilot. He'd seen the terror in the woman's eyes. He'd held the squirming baby in his arms. He understood a little bit better what war was about and that his thoughts were not the same as his governments.

Maybe it was because the men were wounded or because the baby kept crying and the attendants nerves were on edge, he didn't know, but they handled the Vietnamese woman roughly. She no longer cried. Her eyes were on her baby, lest they separate the two. Mark never saw her again. They said she received treatment and left.

The war was involving everyone now. In the following days he watched as the helicopter landed on the pad near the hospital, often carrying victims on stretchers covered in blood head to foot but it was the ones with sheets tucked completely around the bodies that concerned him most. He was sitting on his bunk staring at the floor when Blue walked in.

"You won't believe what I just saw."

"I believe." Mark replied

The war was lasting longer than anyone thought. Mark was out in the woods everyday wondering that the ravaged world around him still had foliage to conceal him when suddenly his power to think, at all, was gone. Something was wrong. What happened? He was slipping away and no one would know.

A tunnel stretched before him. Long and dim, a light seemed to ebb from the farthest point. Hands were tapping his body, shaking his shoulders as his head lolled forward. His head was so heavy he couldn't respond. Then there was nothing but darkness. Lauren? Where are you? Was that him on a table?

"Mark." A woman's voice demanded he respond but he couldn't. A black fog was rolling in.

"Mark?" A man's voice sounded, brisk, commanding. "Buchanan? Buchanan?" He tried to reply from the tunnel. He was no longer lying on the table as he struggled to overcome the blackness; beyond the fog was a light. Could this be real? He could not speak. He wanted to cry out and then he heard his name. Gentle. His body settled. His mind cleared. Mark. He smiled. There was soft laughter. Who spoke? You know who I am. All the fears disappeared. Again, a chuckle. Peace he had not known enveloped his body, his mind turned curious; the surroundings were not anything he had seen before. It was the warmth, the welcoming atmosphere and the voice saying his name with love that brought a feeling of joy that filled his mind and heart. He wanted to stay. Not this time, Mark, the voice said gently.

They contacted his parents. He had tripped while on duty in the woods, a jagged wire so successfully concealed had ripped the flesh on his leg to the bone, and severed an artery. He heard them say he had bled out. What did that mean? Seven minutes. Dead. He's gone. Mark heard them. He felt nothing. He had gone through the tunnel. He was on the other side.

"We have notified the authorities. They will notify his parents, probably working on it now as we speak."

Seven minutes. Wasn't that a lucky number or was it from the bible and meant conclusion? He stared at the white sheet covering his face. Why would they cover his face? They said he was dead. Lauren? I need you, Lauren. They are coming for my body. What will I do? I can hear them but they can't hear me. He was above the gurney, looking down on rows of white wrapped bodies. White? He questioned. Attendants were in the room. "This one was brought in from the field with that one. They worked on him seven minutes before declaring him. This one was dead on arrival, just had to be cleaned up."

"Heart stopped on the operating table. They don't know if he had an allergic reaction or what. I was in there, removing another body. They hit him with the paddles. Did CPR. I saw them glance at the clock. When they do that, you know they've lost their patient."

Don't take me out. Mark couldn't get his tongue to form words. Nothing was working; his hands or feet and certainly not his mouth. *Don't take me. Please don't take me. Lauren? Help me. I need you.*

Sarah had awakened from sleep to slide from the covers onto her knees and now she stood staring out the window where silver moonbeams lay long shadows between the tall pines.

"What's wrong?" John asked, alarmed to find her there.

"It's Mark," She replied. "Something's terribly wrong. He's dying."

Hurriedly, John was doing the time between the states and Vietnam. "It's a dream." He cradled her to his body. "Come back to bed, Sarah. Everything will be better in the morning. It's just a dream."

"No, John. Mark's in trouble. I just heard the word pound through my head. He's dead."

When the phone rang, the next day, she was hesitant to answer, yet drawn to lift it from its cradle.

"Your son almost died last night. It is our responsibility to tell you, he is recuperating."

"Almost?" She questioned. There was a moment of hesitation and then the explanation.

Chapter Fourteen

Lauren almost hadn't driven down to see her parents. The Buchanan's didn't press her for anything while her own folks did. Then the call came through and her mother handed her the phone. She recognized Sarah's voice and she listened. She was stunned to hear Mark had, to all medical actualities, died, but after a length of time was now in recovery. Grieving in her spirit, she knew the message was intended to be delivered to her but in her absence to Mark's parents. Perhaps it was best; the news came from one who loved him dearly. Mark almost died, from a shot, the first aid of an accident suffered innocently enough while on duty. What were they not telling her?

Going quietly to the room of her childhood, Lauren sat on the bed, considering the information. He was there, in a foreign land amidst trees and fallen leaves in a land thousands of miles away from her. If there were consolation, it would be in knowing Mark's love of nature, the peace he'd sought before leaving as they walked the hill paths hand in hand to rest beneath the scarred pines on his father's land. They had spoken of the months they would be separated and that nothing would change their love. Would that be true? After all he had experienced would Mark find loving her as easy as before?

Time became a waiting game. Soon, Mark would be going home. His body recovered from the medical mistake. He saw the new recruits arrive, green replacements looking young while he felt aged inside, more mentally than physical. The ravages of war had taken their toll; a pain he hoped soon forgotten. He rode home as silent as the day he left. He had lasted. His faith in God had taken on new meaning while his patriotic convictions had taken a severe beating. Disillusionment of the mass returning home, he thought, encouraged by his superior's last brief to keep knowledge obtained to himself. And somewhere in the recess of his mind there was a whisper of something that had happened the night of his dying, a peace he needed, a joy in his spirit, the soft laughter he had heard. He closed his eyes, tuned in to the yearnings of his heart. You know who I am. Yes. I know.

It was nineteen seventy one. Without fanfare the air transport arrived. At 3 a.m., he was at Travis Airforce Base in California. He was in the states. Mark was elated. By noon he was sitting with his duffel at Scott Air Force Base, Illinois, waiting for the AF to figure out some ground transport.

Mark began the hike across country in order to beat the delay in transportation the Air Force offered. Wearing dress blues, he was picked up by an old gentleman whose grandson had worn the same. "Where you heading?"

"To Poplar Bluff, Missouri."

"I'll take you there," the old man was changing lanes, taking an exit that would take them the right direction. Against Mark's protest, he said, "My boy didn't return. You did. It seems to me someone should be happy to deliver you wherever you want to go."

Hours later they pulled onto Highway sixty seven. "I'll be heading a different direction, son. Let me know how you are making it, after a while. God bless you." He offered his hand. "Have a good life."

"You, too, sir." Mark smiled; the happiness of being near his family was overwhelming. "God bless you."

"Your hair." Julie exclaimed. "What happened? It's curly." She was hugging him, with a huge kiss upon his cheek while Lauren stood grinning. Now with Brent in her arms Lauren was wearing an expression of uncertainty Julie would wonder about later.

"Maybe the climate over there." The grin spread across his features. "I do believe you are glad to see me." He pecked a kiss on his sister's cheek and turned to shake Blaine's hand. "Man. Two little ones, how does that feel? Here, let me hold him. He needs to know his uncle. Hello, little one. How are you?"

Riding home, Julie turned to Mark. "He was awful quiet wasn't he, after our greeting each other?"

"Maybe he needs a time of transition. Everything appears to be different, culture, daily expectations."

"They have to go to Colorado to finish his time. I think, maybe, Lauren hoped they would stay here."

Colorado has beautiful green fir trees, Lauren wrote, and the mountains are beautiful. We love it here. I think this is a healing balm for the three of us. There's so much ahead of us. Mark will have to find a job, but with the economy we've heard no one is hiring. We have to make the most of our time *here*. Then we will be back with family.

Finishing his time in service, Mark brought his family back to Missouri. He had inquired about his old job. It was no longer available. Withdrawn and tense with adjustments; reinstating his family back into the mainstream of life was more difficult than either he or Lauren had imagined. He needed a job, badly. Traveling to Springfield, Mark underwent the test enabling him to sell Insurance. Selling was one thing, the people able to pay the premiums was another. Though the agency promised profit if he would stay, Mark saw the future as futile and made the decision to seek employment elsewhere.

"I thought the government guaranteed you a job of equal pay and status. Didn't I hear that somewhere?"

"Beats me." Mark replied. "If they did, they didn't mean it. I'm down to finding a job on a farm and Blaine knows I'm ill equipped for that." It was embarrassing. When he left it was a flush market; returning to a pinched economy and a stalemate for veterans seeking work. Finally, after months of searching with their funds dwindling daily, Mark took a job on a farm near Blaine.

"I wish I could've hired you, Mark, but I'd had to fire Bill."

Mark grinned, good-naturedly. "When you consider how long he's been with you and his skill, I don't think you want to do that. Don't worry about it." He paused. "You know, Blaine, it worries me that Lauren has to leave the baby with her parents while she goes to work at the shoe factory."

"They'll fall in love with him and you won't have a worry at all."

Mark's stint at farming began with the Lesley's. Lesley's wife, Pearly, was the main stay of the old man's life. "She literally runs the old man, the farm and about everything else they deal with." Mark said. "She asked me to have lunch with them. No need bringing your own, she'd say, when we got plenty."

"I resisted for a while, then one day she says, to me, do you think my-er- ah-," he grinned, *just supply your own curse word* here, "food unclean?"

"Mark Buchanan, I can't believe you said that. Grandma would turn over in her grave."

"You sound just like her. Julie I'm just repeating what the boss lady said."

"Go on." Blaine insisted, laughing.

"Well, I stuttered around a bit, scratched my toe in the dirt and tried to think up something. Then she says, you know what we're having for lunch? I just shook my head. Fried chicken, gravy, mashed potatoes, fresh peas and black berry cobbler for dessert."

"I was so taken back, she cursed in every sentence, but I'll spare you that. 'I sure as, *curse word here*, know how to cook, she said, just as well as I know where the spark plugs and filter are on that tractor you're driving.' Well, I'd used every excuse I could have, so I went in." He let out a deep breath. "The house was clean, food on the table. Foolishly I asked, "Do you eat like this every day?"

"Yes," she said cursing again. "Now sit there by Bull."

I looked around to see what she was calling Bull.

"Your boss," she explained. "That's what I call him. He's just another bull in heat."

"I nearly choked my tongue. Old man Lesley just grinned and picked up his fork, when she said, 'Bull, I believe this man says grace.' I started to tell her I was out of practice. Suddenly she says, 'Foods getting cold,' and she looks toward heaven and says, 'Bless the damn food."

"I heard the stories," Blaine said, grinning, "But I always wondered if the person telling them just wanted a colorful story."

"She's colorful all right but I think I near exhausted her through that meal, her trying to keep from cussing and me from hearing it.

When I left the table that day I was so agitated I didn't know if I'd eaten or not. Makes the adrenalin start up."

"Maybe she'll change."

"I doubt it." Mark thought for a moment. "No. She won't," he stated firmly.

Christmas arrived, harvest spent, money scarce. The rains had slowed harvest and profits were lean. Still, there were gifts for three little ones under the tree. They'd gathered at John and Sarah's in the hills. In spite of Julie's wanting to prevent her mother all the work, John said, "We're not leaving the house, Julie, girl, so you best pack your bib and tucker and come on home. We ask Bill and Letty and Joe Lynn, too."

Mark viewed the huge pine he and Lauren had dragged down the hill. His father would have settled for the scraggly one at the foot of the hill. "Dad," it's not as if there were too many to pick from. We're going to have this good one." He heard John say, it would mess up his sinuses.

"Then it won't matter whether it's pretty or ugly, short or tall, will it?" Mark mumbled, despairingly, while Lauren giggled quietly into her scarf. "Your mother wanted to put up the silver tree so there wouldn't be any needles dropping."

"I'll clean them up, myself. That silver tree looks like a plucked chicken." Walking over to Lauren, he put his arms around her to pull her close and nuzzle her neck. "You happy, honey?" She nodded. "How can you be? I didn't get you anything for Christmas."

"You're here. It's all I need.

The family together. One by one, Mark studied them, his family. He was home. Surely life would become normal in the months ahead. Mom had never wanted nor seemed to expect other than to be a wife and mother. Olive skinned, the fine lines were tracing time on her face, the dark hair showing streaks of grey. She loved John Buchanan of the fiery temperament and unrest of the soul. Grandma used to say he couldn't help it, he had longed for his father's presence in his life to the point he ran roughshod through life unaware of the blessings poured down on him, intent on his need for his father.

At the moment Mark's father was sitting by Lissie. John was white haired now, bending to watch as Lissie colored, with Lissie explaining the art of staying in the lines to his own son and Brent taking to Lissie much as a sponge to water. Dark haired, dusky lashes on her cheeks and sweet natured, Lissie seemed older than her years. And his father, more patient, happily watching the interaction of the day, smiled and bragged on Lissie and Brent.

His memory quickened; some things were not easily forgotten and he wished not to remember on this day. But there was one missing, Grandma was not present. "The Lord is in the high places, Mark." Her voice came across the ages, as real today as those painful years, "It's not ours to question, son, the Lord knows what he's doing. If you have trials they will make you a better person." Now, he questioned what she had said. "If we don't understand, the least we can do is keep our faith that in the end his plan will work out. I've wondered if trials we encounter are often for the use of other people."

"How's that, Grandma?" His childish voice had asked, "How can other people use our problems?"

"By the way we handle our self through those trials, we either encourage or discourage them to work their way through their own."

"I don't want to go through bad times just so other people can learn from me, Grandma."

She had smiled and patted his knee. "I know, Mark, sometimes I feel like I've been the scapegoat for others, myself."

"What's a scapegoat, Grandma?"

"In biblical times, on the day of atonement, the priest would turn loose a goat signifying the sins of the people were laid upon it and when Jesus died on the cross for our sins he became the scapegoat for us."

"I don't like that either, Grandma. Jesus was without blame. It was wrong for him to have to take the burden of what we do wrong."

"Without Jesus dying on the cross for us, Mark, we would have no salvation."

In his mind, her explanations come down through the ages, and some of it he still didn't understand. He sighed. "Just accept his plan, Mark." He missed her. It was a day of celebration and he sat there missing her as his thoughts sped on to the call God placed on mankind, of acceptance or rejection. Life.

"Look in Isaiah," Myrtle Buchanan would say. "Here, I'll help you." The two of them had searched scripture. "Chapter forty one and forty two; Behold, the former things are come to pass and new things do I declare; before they spring forth, I tell you of them. Listen to this, Mark. When the poor and needy seek water and there is none and their tongue faileth for thirst, I the Lord will hear them. I, the God of Israel will not forsake them. I will open rivers in high places and fountains in the midst of the valleys. I will make the wilderness a pool of water and the dry land springs of water." He remembered how she would glance up to stare into the distance. "Somewhere, it says there will be springs in the desert."

"What does that mean, Grandma?"

"Oh, that's a wonderful work; There's nothing our Lord can't take care of. Our only requirement is faith. We must believe in Him."

Mark's own Bible fell open to a scripture he liked. "The poor man cried and the Lord heard his cry."

"And saved him out of his troubles," Grandma added. "Psalm thirty four, I forget which verse."

Mark shook his head. How many times did this happen? Scripture, he thought forgotten came through his memory. It was as though Grandma sat beside him. He glanced up to see his father's gaze upon him. "Dad, why don't we all go to church together, tomorrow?"

"We'll see, son. I don't always know how I'll feel the next day."

Lauren felt the sag of Mark's body against hers. "We'll go."

"I'd like to go, too," Sarah spoke softly. "We've so much to be thankful for."

Though his head was bowed, Mark felt them, his family gathered on this holy day. *Christmas at home. God bless America.* He felt a draft of pain. Would they always be together?

Julie came to sit with him a minute. "Were you yawning or smiling, Mark?"

"This is the best Christmas ever, Julie, and though I miss Grandma I hear her speaking in my head. She would love it, too. Look, Julie," he smiled. "Our tree turned out beautiful. We didn't have to have a lot of gifts because we have each other and hearts are pure this year."

Julie started to protest. "Well, Lissie may be feeling a bit limited, but the rest of us…our being together is the best gift ever. We will never forget it."

Flipping through channels, Mark listened. The agricultural channel had listed the previous year as one of the wettest in history and there was fear the next would not be better. How could they forecast a bleak future? Rain beat on the windows. Lauren was at the plant, their son with her mother as he watched the hands on the clock creep slowly around.

Combing through his hair, longer now, he sighed. Maybe it was a rebellious act against time and command; His dad didn't like it and he was the one asked the question. "What does Lauren think of your new style?" Lauren didn't care, she understood anything was long after the shaved head of being in service. Time weighed heavily on his shoulders. If he wasn't working, he developed a guilt trip that he wasn't better providing for his family. Lauren rode to work with the neighbor and helped pay for the gas. He climbed into the old wagon and headed toward Julie's. It was two hours until Lauren arrived home.

"Where you been, Bub?" Julie closed the door quickly behind them. "Is this a North westerner?" Wind and rain was lashing at the door. She motioned for him to take a seat.

"It's something," he grinned, "But I don't know that word for sure."

"Come on, let's set at the table. Blaine will be home before long."

"I hope so, the old clunker sounds strange and I was hoping he'd listen to it."

"You've been busy, huh?"

"Still working with the Lesley's," Mark sighed. "But this rain. Three days now. No work, no pay."

"Nothing's opening up?" Already, Julie sensed he was feeling down.

"I interviewed for another job with an insurance agency, this morning. I figure I got the training, maybe I can sell insurance on the side." His eyes held hers; there was a twinkle in his. "When it rains."

"You are willing to try that again?" She stared at Mark's hair, longer and curling. That amazed her.

"What can I do, Julie? If it rains as much as it did while we were trying to harvest, my family can't live destitute. Lauren's working won't pay all the bills and I can't just sit home thinking things will get better."

It appeared things were looking up. After he explained to Pearly what his plans were, Mark moved his family out of the drafty old house the Lesley's provided. Lauren explained the situation to Julie, her eyes dancing as she told the story.

"She appeared in our yard the next morning. I could hear the cursing through the door and peeped out the window, making sure I didn't move the curtain." She giggled. "She wasn't happy Mark was leaving. She had thought on it through the night. New Year wasn't even started, she said, and here he was leaving. Oh, the profanities were rolling through the air."

"Only moving," Mark explained. "I plan to sell insurance on the days it rains. I'll be back."

"No you won't and I already received your rent. I guess you expect that back?" Pearly asked.

"What's that, thirty dollars?" Lauren inquired.

Lauren nodded. "Oh, Julie, I wish you could have heard, it took me awhile to figure out she was actually telling him he was the best, uh-blank- blank hand they'd had and they hated to lose him. I could see her through the crack and her mouth was moving, ever-other-word a curse word. "Whose gonna bless our food?" she said and when I saw Mark laughing I decided I had to meet his boss. Enough time had passed. You would have thought we were moving to China."

"I surely would like to meet her. Could she be put in print? She sounds like a real character."

"No, the page would smolder."

The day before they moved, Mark appeared. "Julie, let's go put flowers on Grandma's grave."

Leaving Blaine a note, Julie left with Mark. Blaine Jr. sat in the back seat enjoying the scenery.

"The earth is changing," Mark said. "Did I hear you say, umm? What does that mean? Are you, down, Julie?" He peered at her, tilting his head as he glanced back at the road, waiting. "What is it?"

"I start work at the newspaper, next week."

"Really?" He was excited for her. "Then why so glum?"

"I hate putting my baby in Daycare and leaving Blaine to do all the work, just him and Bill when I was helping. Of course Lissie is very vocal saying she is too old for a baby sitter; she will ride the bus home."

"Then why are you doing it?"

"Finances. It rained so much last year, we profited very little, meaning one of us had to get an outside job." She turned to face him. "How could Blaine make a living for not only us but Mom and Dad if he left the farm every day?"

"I see what you mean, the farm makes a living for two families; owner of the farm and the guy farming it. Guess I don't think along the right lines all the time." He reached over to squeeze her hand. "You'll be good, Julie. What will you do at the Newspaper?"

"There's a column they want me to handle, but mostly I'll go out with a camera and find people with interesting lives and a story to tell. They said that draws people in and keeps their circulation up."

"That's great, Julie. Maybe you can tell some of your stories and end with the words you always told me; *they received all the golden promises*. What will you call your column?"

"I don't know. They probably have that all figured out."

"If they don't, I think you should name it Promises. Don't let those stories go to waste, Julie."

Chapter Fifteen

Weekly visits were a ritual for Julie, but now she went on Saturday. Dad would be in the pasture mending fences and Mom in the kitchen. On this day she arrived to find the door to the kitchen open. Angry voices carried to where she stood. She heard Mark's name mentioned. He had been at her house last evening. He seemed troubled but refused to share what he was fretting over.

"Three thousand dollars? From a Finance company?" John Buchanan's voice snapped through the air, harsh, angry and cold. John Buchannan cursed. "Why didn't he come to me?"

"Mark has pride." The gentle voice of her mother replied.

The crash of a fist on the table, followed by cracking sounds of dishes hitting the floor greeted Julie.

"What's wrong?" She stood in the doorway surveying the scene. Her dad was angry, Sarah was pale.

Her father rounded the room, his mouth twisted into an ugly shape, a sheaf of papers in one hand, held over her head. "Your brother. Wait until I get my hands on him."

Sarah Buchanan began to sob, lines of pain settling in her face and her eyes grew dim as she twist the apron she was wearing in her hands. Julie stared at them. "He came to my house yesterday. I felt something was wrong but he couldn't tell me. You said something's wrong? I knew it then but I couldn't get him to say what it was." Hysteria rose inside of Julie. "Mom, call Lauren. See if he's there."

Her mother dialed, her fingers balking clumsily missing the numbers at first, then having asked for Mark, she turned to face them. "He's gone. Lauren said he didn't come home, yesterday. She was crying. She said Mark left a note saying he was sorry. He had to leave to try to find a better life for them."

Weeks turned into months. John Buchanan paced the floor and he had no appetite. Lauren went through the motion of living. She didn't speak words of fault or blame. Julie wondered all the while, what were they hiding? Why would Mark leave. Her heart ached remembering how sad he looked the day he visited and it went round in her mind, why couldn't he tell her what was bothering him?

Then, Sarah called. Lauren was taking Brent and going to join Mark. At least, she thought, he has a job. It would have been hard for Mark, to face their father. John Buchanan paid off the loan and with Sarah's guidance tried to stifle the anger that resided in him over the incident. Julie wondered was it his pride hurt that Mark had not borrowed from him, or the fact his son had to borrow. She and Mark never spoke of the matter, it was best for all for him to think no one knew.

The years passed with the children growing and Julie working at the newspaper. Sometimes when news was nil, she actually offered a few of her stories. According to the editor, Julie was developing a following that waited for her latest column.

"You're helping sell subscriptions."

Thinking out loud, Julie said, "Then I suppose you will be giving me a raise, huh?"

Julie counted the passing of time watching the children grow. She and Blaine decided to keep the family ties intact; someone had to move beyond John Buchanan's displeasure. They broke the ice by meeting Mark and Lauren on weekends, trying hard to keep the trips equal traveling distance. Mark knowing his mother longed to see his family visited during the holidays when his job permitted.

Julie placed a wreath of roses on Myrtle Buchanan's grave and standing there wished she could have one more talk with her grandmother. *I'm tired, Grandma. I need to be home with my children and Blaine.* She could almost hear a reply. *"Where there's a will, there's a way, Julie girl."*

It was almost time for wheat harvest. "We need to get away a few days, why don't we see if your brother's family can join us. We can rent a cabin with enough bedrooms to sleep all of us."

Julie made the call and waited for Lauren to contact Mark to see if they could drive the two hundred miles and meet at the lake that was almost half way for both families. Everything was arranged. A call confirmed the cabin, and a frenzied packing of supplies began.

The children's anticipation was amusing. They were excited to be away for a brief time and excited to be together. From the moment they arrived they realized the time would fly by and they would head home. During the day they floated down the river and swam in the deepest water. Nearby there was a lake but the children were content with the rivers stream and the rope high in the tree they could swing out on. By dark the children were tiring down and subdued. Then they sat around the campfire, wrapped in blankets Julie and Lauren had brought for settling into the swings provided by the cabin owner.

"It's so pleasant here," Lauren said. "Who knew we'd be enjoying each other. I wasn't sure we could come. Thank you both for asking us."

"Did you see the grave yard, just before you turned? It was tucked into that hill side. Pretty neat."

"I saw it," Mark nodded. "When I die, I'd like to be buried on a hillside that looks down into a valley."

Shivering at the thought, Julie asked, "Why? Does it matter where we're buried, once we're gone?"

"Think about it. On a hill side looking down." He reached across and tweaked Julie's nose.

"I'd rather not think about that. There's really no need for people's suffering before death."

"It comes to all, part of life," Mark replied. "Did you see the sail boat out on the lake?"

"Missed that," Blaine replied. "I doubt we could rent a sail boat but we could rent a pontoon. What do you think?"

"Sounds good. Maybe we should turn in early so we can get full day's benefit of the pontoon." Mark glanced at his sister. "But before we go, let's let our roving reporter tell us at least one of her famous stories with promise."

"What's promise, Daddy?" Brent asked.

"When I was little, Aunt Julie told me stories to help the time pass more quickly and get my mind off whatever chore we were doing and she always ends the story saying the people received all the golden promises, which meant there were good things planned for their life."

"I'm out of practice. Maybe I don't believe in all the promises, anymore."

"Well, I do." Mark replied. "Tell us a story, Julie." Mark tucked Brent to his side and waited for her to begin.

"Once upon a time, long ago there was a forest. All around the forest lay lush fertile land. To this land came a man and his wife. "Here, I will build a farm," the good man declared in his firm voice. "I will make a home," the woman replied softly. They began to toil, day and night. The seasons changed from Springs green to summer's bright blinding sun, to fall with leaves blowing through the air; until winter arrived chasing the man and woman inside the home they had built together. From the window they watched as winter winds howled, the trees were bare with limbs that pointed to the sky like so many fingers. But the trunks of the trees became shelter for tiny animals that roamed the forest. "We've worked hard," the man said. "Now we can sit by the fire together and stay warm." Air swooshed down the chimney and whistled around the corners of the house but they were safe inside.

Little by little, tiredness left the man's body and at last his stern countenance relaxed as a slight smile touched his mouth until finally his eyes crinkled at the corner and twinkled within and he said, "My dear, you have made me very happy. Is there anything you long for to make you happier?" Then he called her Sarah, which means Princess, because he was tired of saying my good woman or my dear. This woman he called Sarah named him, John, which means God's gift."

"That's my grandma and Poppa's name," Brent exclaimed, while everyone laughed.

"Many days," Sarah said, "You labor in the fields and I'm alone in the house. I would be most happy if there were children playing around my feet. "A son, to help me work," John replied. "Yes, a child." In time, the woman bore a child. The man paced the floor waiting to hear a baby's cry and finally the cry was heard. Going to the room, he peered down into the bed where the baby lay and it was not a son but a daughter. "Never you mind, in time I shall give you a son," she said. He loved the girl, anyway."

"Aunt Julie, did the man really love the little girl since he wanted a little boy?"

"Yes, he did, Brent."

"Years passed. The man was kind to his daughter and he worked hard to care for his family. He worked so hard he became impatient in small things because he was responsible for many large things and he was becoming very tired."

"Why was he impatient, Aunt Julie?"

"He wasn't one to waste time, therefore those who did disturbed him." Julie laughed. Brent was trying hard to understand. "Shall I quit or go on, Brent?"

"Didn't he ever do something fun, like go fishing?" He was thinking hard but said, "Go on, Aunt Julie."

"Yes, he did. But the good man was changing. His bright blue eyes were not as bright and on the inside where no one could see why, the man saw and felt things differently than the rest of his family."

"Why, Aunt Julie?"

"No one knows why, Brent, but right about then his wife, Sarah, gave birth to a son and she named him Mark."

"That's you, Daddy. The little boy has your name."

"Now the father will forget the little girl," Lissie said. "Just wait and see." She glared at her brother.

"John's mother lived down the road and she decided to keep an eye on the girl and teach the little boy to memorize scripture."

"See," Lizzie nodded her head. "I told you. Everyone likes the boy better than the girl"

"She didn't say the little boy went with his daddy and did all the good things," Brent declared. "Did you, Aunt Julie?"

"Remember, the daddy had a lot to do and he was still impatient and couldn't always take the boy with him."

"John and Mark," Brent said. "Right?" Everyone nodded.

"The grandmother is turning the boy into a wimp. I can just see it." Lissie's voice throttled.

"Wimp?" Blaine grinned at his daughter. "Is that word in the dictionary?"

"But remember, the boy stayed with his grandmother, a lot, and learned scripture. She loved him very much." Julie drew the children closer to her side. "She taught the boy by using the Bible. She prepared him for manhood by using the bible."

"Like David and Goliath?" Brent questioned, now that he was drawn into the story. "He was anointed by the Lord, wasn't he Mommy?" Lauren nodded and smiled, that was her boy.

"Through her love for the boy, the independent old woman's heart was softened. "There are promises here," she would remind the boy as she laid her hand on the bible. "You must claim them as you go through life."

"Did the girl believe that, too?" Lissie's eyes searched her mother's, "Or did she have a mind of her own? That's what you tell me when I don't want to do what you say, isn't it?"

"No, sad to say, the girl did not always claim those promises in the Bible. She was like you and me, sometimes she made up other stories, but in the end she would remember her grandmother's words and whoever she told her stories to, she always said 'and the end of the story is this,' they claimed all the golden promises."

Mark clapped his hands together. "Good job, sis."

"A bit longer than I intended. Sorry, had to stop and answer questions." She grinned. "It's o.k."

"Was that really about Cinderella?" Lissie stood before her, head tilted, reminding Julie of her self at that age. Julie sighed, her own daughter was as belligerent as she had been. It was payback.

"I suppose the girl thought of it as Cinderella," Julie replied. "Her heart longed for fairy tales and she heard a lot of bible scripture, but it all worked out in the end."

"Why do you think Grandma was so strong willed, Julie?" Mark asked.

"I think because she was the provider for her family. Life wasn't easy but Grandma was determined her children would have the best she could give them and she truly believed they needed God in their lives. You should know, Mark. Grandma loved you."

"And Dad?" Mark allowed himself to glance around the circle. The children had slipped off, he could see them sitting inside the small tent Julie brought for the children's play. His eyes lingered on Lauren. They had needed this time away with Julie and Blaine. "Why were things so hard, Julie, growing up? Was I the reason Dad was tense or was Dad's…" He paused, collecting his thoughts. "How do I say this; the problem between myself and Dad, what caused it?"

"You know," Julie sought fairness in trying to help Mark understand. "Grandma tried to explain Daddy's loss, to me. Remember the tractor episode?" Her brother nodded. "It cut her to the bone when she found out. I don't know if she talked to him about it, but she said it wasn't right and her worry was if it continued, the relationship between you and Dad would worsen and you would leave before it was time." Julie sighed, "That's what daddy did with her. He would never accept Grandma trying to tell him she couldn't travel the country with his father doing his carpenter work, with six boys at various ages, full of mischief, riding on her skirt tail. Dad held it against her. He wanted so badly to be near his father."

"What did that have to do with me?" Mark's expression was that of a hurt little boy. Lauren's hand tightened around his and he was grateful for her caring. "He wanted his father when he was a boy. He had me and that was what I wanted."

"I know, Mark." Julie's heart ached as the years came crashing around them as though it were yesterday. "Was it every day, Mark, or on occasion those times happened? We were kids and all I know is we felt sad when they happened; you, mom and me."

"It felt like every day, Julie. I was a boy and it seemed to become harder when I reached an age that I was old enough and large enough in body to work; we grew into a problem of me not knowing what was expected of me." He sighed, his voice wandering back through the years. "I never understood."

"Grandma tried to explain so much to me, Mark. I know it was because she felt the same pain over dad that Mom felt over you and Dad was having trouble; they were caught in the middle and she wanted someone to know why."

"Did it make the problem go away, Julie?"

"What about the book we read, Mark?" Lauren asked, "Has Julie read that book?" Embarrassed, Mark pulled his hand away. "It's about relationships, Julie," Lauren explained. "Parent-child, wives and husbands, the stages we all work through."

"I'm interested. What did you glean from it about the parent child situation?"

"I remember what stood out for me," Mark said. "In early life a child comes to the conclusion that his parent is all right but he isn't. And I wondered, as a child what my flaw was. The book says the way the child feels begins to influence everything he thinks and does, thereafter."

"Well, there's nothing jaded or sinister about you, Mark. How do you explain that?"

"It was Mom and Grandma's love and I know Grandma teaching me to look for wisdom in the Bible accounts for how I look at things. When I'm in doubt, even now as an adult, I hear the whisper of the Holy Spirit and a bible passage comes to mind."

"Then you don't hold Dad responsible?"

"I didn't say I was a saint," Mark grinned, his laughter following, infectious and good. "Nah, I know Dad loves me. I give him credit. He was trying to beat sense into my hard head."

"And you love Dad," Julie said softly, her eyes on her brother. "I really love you, Bub."

"I know. It's mutual." Everyone was smiling. "Life is good, not financial free, but good most the time."

Chapter Sixteen

Those words would come to mind in the future. Wheat harvest was upon them; Blaine was short of help, the sun was rising in the sky and he was itching to start the combine, but a shower past midnight prevented doing so. "If there's no dew, we'll work past midnight." He was staring out the window, "Truly wheat does appear as the song says golden waves of grain." He sighed, "And everything's determined in our world by the weather. We need another hand. We're all so tired, I keep cautioning the men to be fully alert; when you're tired like this, accidents can happen. Take time and think it through."

"If you plan on Lissie working today, I'll need to waken her." With a troubled expression, Julie continued. "She's still a child, Blaine. And she's getting worn thin."

Blaine grinned. "She's not half bad out there; she could drive the combine with a few instructions."

"Don't you dare." Julie stopped stacking dishes at the sink "Is she really that good?"

"Yeah, she is. Mark wasn't much older when I taught him to drive the combine."

"As I recall, Bill broke an arm or leg, which was it? He has suffered through both. Anyway, Dad needed a driver and you told him Mark was capable and Dad was in for a shock because Mark was."

"I'll never forget the look on your dad's face. I think that was a good time between them."

Julie didn't relate what Bill and Letty told her later. Letting it slide she asked, "Why hasn't Mark been around lately?"

"He was down at Bill and Letty's the last time they were home. We didn't see them that week end."

"Hmm. That means Mark is deliberately staying away, then something's wrong."

"And you would dig it out of him, wouldn't you?" Blaine pulled her against his body. "You would."

"It has to be about money. You heard him say his job wasn't what was promised."

"Julie," Blaine cautioned, turning her to look into his eyes. "Don't borrow trouble. It comes on its own." He knew she would push away, but he wouldn't let go. "We're all right, Julie. It comes in and goes back out. So don't transfer Mark's problems to us. We should have a little left over."

"But not enough to help Mark," Julie sighed. "That's the brunt of life, isn't it? Life's a gamble." She had plans for the day but now they weren't important. "I wish we could help Mark."

"He hasn't asked." Blaine headed toward the door. "Send Lissie out about ten o'clock. She will work all day just to drive that old truck and that's a big help." Pausing, with the door half opened, Blaine stared at her. "Julie, you have to let a man do the best he can before he starts asking for help."

"I told Grandma I'd never marry a farmer."

Blaine grinned. "She was a grand old girl; I remember her telling you numerous times to pay attention to what I was saying. She liked me." Chuckling he shut the door as the dish cloth made a soft thud and slid down it.

Now, his eyes scanned the horizon for a hint of cloud. Stepping briskly toward the shop he knew they would run the combine with lights that night. With a deep breath, he was ready for the day, but a niggle of despair over Mark's situation remained in his thoughts. He had to let them simmer on the back burner, as he told the men; they all had to keep their mind on the business at hand. But seeing Mark doubled over, the weekend they were at the cabin, made him wonder if there were more problems. "Don't tell Julie," Mark had said. "She'd just worry. I think I'm developing Dad's kind of stomach."

The news came and it wasn't good.

"Mark lost his job. He said he was the last hired and the first to go." Sarah explained. "They're moving back. He's found a job with that welding company just outside town; the one that erects those steel buildings." Sarah sighed. "Your dad's happy. Maybe this time there won't be trouble."

"Where will they live?" This was news that left Julie with a lot of questions.

"The Burrows are moving. You know our neighbors whose daughter died of the aneurysm? When your dad told them Mark's coming back they asked if Mark and Lauren would want to live in their house. They just want someone to keep an eye out for the few livestock. Mark said he would."

"If Lauren works, you may be ask to keep Brent." Julie searched her mother's face. "Are you up to it?"

"I welcome the thought. I wish I could keep them all." Sarah walked closer to the window to see John and Julie's little son hand in hand walking along the fence that divided the garden from the cattle. "Come, Julie. See your dad and your son? Now isn't that a picture?"

"What's worrying you, Mom?" She felt this underlying sorrow in her mother and questioned why?

"Truth, Julie?" Those serious gray eyes met her daughter's and the words would be imprinted on their minds for eternity. "I worry about losing your dad. The doctor said the cancer is taking hold. He's coughing more and I worry about Mark. I don't know if it was what he suffered as a child or what he saw in Vietnam but there's a part of him closing off from me. He doesn't want to worry me. Julie, but I'm the mother. When our children experience heart ache, we had rather know what it is than worry and wonder." She let her head droop for a moment to stare at the floor. "I count on you a lot, Julie. We've always been friends even though we're mother and daughter. If there are problems, tell me."

Julie reached out and brought her mother into her arms for a hug. "I'm all right Mom. My family's well. We struggle financially but that's because the weather has been against us. I figure you and Dad know all about that. You don't have to worry about us, Mom. Mark wouldn't want you suffering like this over him, either."

Everyone pitched in to settle Mark and Lauren into the Burrows home. It was in need of paint and the carpets had been removed to reveal hard wood floors beneath which John said needed a good sanding. "There's nothing wrong that can't be fixed," Mark agreed. "At least it's clean and it's free." He beamed.

"See, Mom," Julie whispered, "You got your man and your boy within hollering distance and you can let not your heart be troubled, as Grandma probably taught Mark. I heard that somewhere."

Smiling, Sarah replied, "she would say to you, just now, don't be irreverent on the scripture, girl."

Mark began work immediately and the Buchannan and their kin, as Julie explained it, were happy. Lauren found employment as a secretary for Moses real Estate. With her first months' salary, they were able to find a car within reach of their budget.

Chapter Seventeen

It was another year of harvest. "I'm tired, Mom. I just want to stay home." Lissie slumped into a chair.

"You should change jobs," she complained, "so you can be home, more."

"To help your father by doing what you have been doing, I suppose?"

"Well, yeah."

"Elizabeth Dawn, I've heard enough complaining. I'm tired, too, and your father is about ready to fall on his face." She slammed the plate onto the sink, to hear a cracking sound as the plate divided. "Do you see what just happened?"

"It's not my fault."

"Lissie, please. We're all tired. You will be going back to school soon, can't you help your father. He's worn to the bone."

"Don't call me, Lissie. I hate that name. Everyone else has modern names but for me, it's Lissie this, Lissie that. I hate it."

Turning from the sink, Julie stared at her daughter, seeing a part of herself at that age while already the tears were running down Lissie's cheeks. The dusky lashes reminded her of Mark and the sadness of his childhood. "I'm sorry, honey." She crossed the room to put her arms around her daughter, feeling the resistance but she wouldn't let go, she held tight, kissing Lissie's forehead. "Of course it wasn't your fault. I dropped it. We're all so tired, sweetheart. But what about your Dad? He counts on you."

"When can I sleep late, Mom?"

"It looks like rain, any minute, if it doesn't pass us by again." She watched as a resigned Lissie headed back to her room and Blaine entered. "Today's Saturday, maybe you can catch a nap tomorrow evening, after church."

"What's up? Was she crying?"

"Honestly, if it doesn't rain soon, we may all kill each other."

"I know what you mean." He slumped onto the chair. "Too many hours working, nerves on edge; I think we have lived this year after year but surely we had a few good ones in between, didn't we?"

"If we didn't," she replied, sitting across from him, "Someone should shoot us." Lightning flashed in the sky, the sound of a gunshot, making her jump. "Was that lightening or a gun?"

Blaine laughed. "All I know is we both jumped and I saw the lightening. Sounded like it hit something."

"I have clothes on the line. It was too pretty to stick them in the dryer."

"Let me help you," he said, "I hope we don't get killed saving the electric bill for a load of clothes."

After checking to see everyone was in safe from the storm, Lissie and Blaine Jr., were in their rooms, Julie and Blaine sat down at the table. "I don't know if it was the lightening sounding so close or what but I have this ominous feeling, something's wrong." Julie glanced toward the window, frowning.

"Come on, now," Blaine's expression was pleading. "I never like to hear you say that."

Rain pelted the ground, beat on the windows and remained a downpour for an hour. Ending as quickly as it had come, Blaine opened the door to peer out. "Oh, my God, my God." He was running towards the road as Lissie entered the room.

"Is daddy cursing or praying, Momma?" She spoke as she followed her mother to the door.

Seeing what her husband saw, Julie whispered with a sob in her throat. "He was praying. Daddy was praying."

Blaine's hands were stretched to Heaven. "Oh, Lord, how will I tell Bill and Letty?"

"Is there no help, Blaine?" Tears were streaming down Julie's face as she and Lissie clutched each other's arm. "Go back, Lissie, don't let your brother come out of the house to see this and call 911. Can you do that?" Running toward the house, Lissie was repeating nine-one-one. They were all in shock.

For months after, the community would speak in whispers about Bill and Letty's boy being hit by lightning. Wherever one went that first week, the news was the same. "He was on his new Harley, it all shiny, except where the lightening hit and knocked the paint off. Killed Joe Lynn instantly, the medics said. He never had a chance and him just a mile from home. Don't seem fair, does it?"

The accident altered lives, starting with Julie and Blaine. They'd thought they were faithful in church but losing a friend brought sanction to their lives, something of a renewed oath to the God they served. There was a need to be better people; and in view of Bill and Letty's grief in losing their only child, a vow to help them through the process. It often seemed the other way around, Bill and Letty comforting them.

"I told him it was time he settled down," Bill said, "But him and his missus got a divorce and he gave her everything but his truck, went down to the dealership and traded it in for that motorcycle." Tears ran down Bill's face as he told the story and his thoughts for the millionth time on the matter. Respectful, they listened hoping one day he would tire of the telling. "No grand kids. Just me and Letty to grow old alone," he would say. "You know what my boy said that day? He was ready to start the trip down here, he says Pop, I love you and Mom and I just want to thank you that you never put me through the hell I'm going through with this divorce. If anything ever happens to me, you just remember you've been the best parents a son can have and I love you."

John and Sarah had come that day and Mark and Lauren. Bill asked Mark if he would speak at the funeral. Mark replied, "I'll cry, Bill but I'm honored that you ask me."

"What will you say?" Julie lay her head against Mark's shoulder as he hugged her. She found it difficult to turn loose. She gave the same depth of hug to her parents and to Lauren and Brent. She saw the grayness of her father's skin, knowing it wasn't just the cancer; her father was barely able to stand in view of Bill and Letty's loss. John Buchannan faced his own demons. Mark sensed his father's need, too. Julie knew by the way he hovered near them. It would be heartache to lose either one. For now, her mind switched back. She wondered again what Mark would say about Joe Lynn.

The day of the funeral, Mark stood before the congregation in the Hope Community Church building. The pews were filled and many stood outside listening quietly. Chairs had been set up on the lawn and taken to the last one.

The pastor of the church came forward to give the eulogy. He spoke of Joe Lynn being an only child, of Joe Lynn's outgoing personality and how he was bent to find fun in any situation which was a magnet that drew people to him. And then he turned the service over to Mark. Julie roused from private thoughts concerning her parents and Letty and Bill's suffering to concentrate on her brother.

"May we all rise as we pray the Lord's Prayer." There was a shuffling of feet and the rustle of movement as the people stood. "Our Father who art in Heaven, Hallowed be thy name. Thy kingdom come, Thy will be done on earth as it is in Heaven. Give us this day, our daily bread and forgive us our trespasses as we forgive those who trespass against us; and lead us not into temptation and deliver us from evil, for Thine is the kingdom and the power and the glory forever. Amen.

Hope choir began to sing, the song bringing tears to even the hardest of hearts. And then it was time for Mark to speak. He stood silently looking out onto the friends and neighbors honoring Joe Lynn.

"When we pray," Mark began, "It is important that we understand whether we are God's child or not. When we say, Our Father, we need to understand He is our Heavenly father and He cares for us. When we say Thine is the kingdom and the power and the glory forever, we must understand our Heavenly Father is the Creator, whose greatness spans not only the days of our lives but goes with us into eternity."

"In the bible, Matthew tells us our heavenly Father knows the number of hairs on our head. He knows our needs before we ask. How compassionate is a friend who cares about our needs and even knows the number of hair on our head? Is it important we know whether we are His child? What determines our knowing? If we have been spiritually reborn into His kingdom, just as we were physically born to life and we understand we are without a doubt His child, we can pray the prayer to our Father."

"What have we done to reach that status? We have repented of our sins and ask Him to be our Savior and through that process He has become Our Heavenly Father. With that settled, we turn to the story of Job and we hear Job saying, The Lord gives and the Lord takes away. What does the scripture mean? Job lost everything, ten children, seven thousand sheep, five hundred yoke of oxen and the count goes on. He thought his neighbors would never tire of telling him what to do because of his loss."

"Here is a man of integrity, suffering great loss and it seems he can do nothing about it. But Job had faith, he had strength of character and while others railed against him, Job hung on."

"How many of you remember the boy, Joe Lynn?" Mark smiled as hands went up. "Do you remember Wednesday night church services where we studied scripture and learned about God? Was Joe Lynn present?" Heads were nodding. "Yes, he was. He knew the scripture. Joe Lynn gave his heart to the Lord but Joe Lynn was no stick in the mud. He marched to a different tune than most of us. Joe Lynn knew what he wanted and he stepped out front and got it. I remember Joe Lynn's love to sing the song, "The Ninety and Nine." It became a theme song for us, as we met each week to help with the little children in church," Mark grinned, "And we though only three years older, thought we were men as we sang it."

"That song spoke of the Shepherd, who has ninety nine sheep in the fold, but one is lost and the Shepherd goes in search, at great expense to himself as it is in rugged territory he must travel. And our scripture in Job does not compare to that shepherd, does it? Except Job is a man of exceptional character, and in spite of adversity, he believes. Joe Lynn and I were baptized in this church. He was older than me but he never acted like he was. We did things together. Joe Lynn liked to say the Lord's prayer. He studied the story of Job, trying to understand why God would allow the devil to create havoc in his life. Joe Lynn sang the song of the Ninety and Nine with gusto that would make George Beverly Shea take notice."

"Is it strange that God would inspire men to write a book on suffering and choose, Job, a man of integrity to show us how compassion works? Bill and Letty lost their son. We grieve with them but we cannot know their grief. They must have thought hope was lost for tomorrow but Bill and Letty have already expressed their sentiments on the subject. Like Job, they will praise God even when it is hard and loss buckles them to the floor; they will call on His name and receive comfort. Is it strange a young man like Joe Lynn would choose the Ninety and Nine as a favorite song? Not if you know the song."

"Joe Lynn was my child hood friend. There were probably times I hero worshipped him. He knew what he wanted and he wasn't going to settle for less. He may have been a slow starter where work was concerned but when he found his niche he filled it to capacity and loved the work he was allowed to do."

"Why did his life end in such a horrible way? Joe Lynn was never one who liked fishing, why hurt the fish, he would say, even when he was slapping the water with a makeshift pole. No, he wouldn't hurt the fish. When that bolt of lightning hit Joe Lynn, I believe he entered Heaven and though he was caught off guard and his time come before he planned, I can see him as he looks around and sees the grandeur of Heaven, and says, "Cool."

"I believe Joe Lynn said thank you, for not having prolonged suffering. And if there were windows or doors that were open to see to earth, Joe Lynn was wondering how long until the people he loved will arrive in Heaven so he can greet them; but scripture does not tell us if that is a possibility; what it tells us is to be ready. Joe Lynn lived life to the fullest but once in the heart of a child, he accepted his Savior."

Julie sat with family; Lissie and young Blaine between her and their father. Old habits were hard to break. Grandma had first called her great granddaughter, Lissie and now Lissie wanted to be called Elizabeth. She was growing up. Though she had sweetness within her, Lissie had a streak of independence Julie feared would bring trouble to her young life. It was a new generation. Almost sighing, she turned her attention back to Mark. Several people had stood to tell about Joe Lynn and now Mark was bringing the eulogy to a close. Teresa Tharp was singing the song, "The Ninety and Nine."

Listening, it spoke to Julie's heart as she glanced at her young and vulnerable daughter racing to see the world, a victim of time and changing ethics; an abortion clinic had opened its doors in the adjoining town. Julie shuddered, praying her family never entered those doors. How could she love her daughter enough that she would have the wisdom to remain strong against the pull of the world? The song ended, the shepherd in the song had felt the one lost and fallen sheep worth rescuing from the ravine, though the shepherd was bleeding from each attempt. Julie sighed, she must love her child that much.

"Joe Lynn loved life. Letty. Bill. Joe Lynn would not want you to quit life. I feel if he could give you one last message he would encourage you to go on, to remember the way he embraced people and the world around him. He had not planned to leave those he loved so soon but in his heart he knew the glories of dying and going to the Savior of His soul. When you grieve, remember his laughter. When you ache, remember his hugs, and when you cry, listen for his voice saying Heaven is what we aim for our whole life, we just put it on a back burner, but it is the ultimate goal for a child of the Heavenly Father and Joe Lynn is experiencing all the mysteries of Heaven right now that we can only wonder about."

"Friends," Mark focused on those before him, "Say I'll be there one day," and live your life accordingly as you remember this robust friend who has gone on. Bill and Letty, I believe with all my heart, Joe Lynn is whole and happy and walking by Jesus side. When you get there, there will be rejoicing to see your loved one again but most of all to see Jesus, the Savior of your soul. God bless you all. The family thanks you for coming to pay tribute to the memory of Joe Lynn. May God's peace and His grace bless you as you travel to your home."

Chapter Eighteen

Julie would recall Mark's message in the next weeks, reviewing the sincerity with which he spoke. Was it because Joe Lynn was his friend and he knew the family or had Mark missed his calling? Julie missed the trips to the hills to visit. Life had become busy. With school functions, the farm work a must, and her own job it was all she could do to stay on top. Then she received a call from her mother.

"Julie, Mark's having surgery tomorrow. I thought you would want to know now and not hear it later."

"What's wrong?"

Sarah sighed. "Mark tells me it is nothing more than a hernia operation. Your dad and I are going."

Thinking of the column due the next morning, Julie mentally made a note to finish it that night. "I think I will come up, too. Mark hasn't had many rounds with the doctor, has he?"

"I keep remembering when the officials came to tell us Mark had received medicine he was allergic to and to all purposes died. Even though that is on his record we feel we should be present for him and Lauren's sake. Brent will be in school."

"I'll be there, Mom."

The waiting room was cool on that day in May when Mark was scheduled for a simple hernia operation. Julie waited with Lauren and her parents to receive the report following surgery. Within the first hour the doctor appeared. "Buchanan family?" They all stood.

The doctor wore a troubled expression. "I never envisioned this," he said. "It explains his tiredness the past months." Nervous agitation creased his words. "I would never have thought…" He realized their failure to understand, his voice became more controlled and professional. "He has pancreatic cancer. It's through his whole body." He glanced around the waiting room. "I don't think he will live off of the operating table."

Mark's father reeled, fighting off the anxiety, but his body hit the floor a dull thudding sound on the tiles. Julie saw this as the void rolled up. She was trying to help raise her father; aware of her mother's sobs intermingling with the drone of the vendor machine. And Lauren, blanched as her head sagged to her chest, the thick strands of blonde hair curtaining her face. Cancer. The urge to run flashed through Julie. Cancer. *"He won't live off the operating table."* The words pound in her head. *Cancer. Won't live.*

But he did and when the anesthesia loosened its hold, Mark rallied and the doctor appeared. "Am I all right, Doc?"

"You are for now, son. We'll talk when you come around, good." The doctor didn't leave.

Julie watched him sitting there, still and controlled with his presence emanating a false calm over them. When Mark was fully conscious the words were spoken. Mark seized the doctor with his right hand, trying to raise his body but wincing with pain from the incision while his left hand held the bed sheets so tightly, his fingers were digging down and he was sobbing. Julie turned away as Lauren went to him. Here was a broken man with no hope clinging to his wife.

Thirty years old. Julie's mind tottered between acceptance and denial. The nurse had given him a shot and he might never wake up. Unmerciful the day filed past. Lauren went home to explain to Brent but what do you say to a child? Sitting by Mark's bedside Julie tried to wade through a line of senseless prayer. John and Sarah stood at the foot of the bed until the doctors persuaded them they, too, must rest. Julie checked with Blaine.

"Everything's all right, here," he soothed, "If you feel you need to stay longer. Then stay."

Kindness came from unexpected quarters. A friend from their childhood had heard Mark was in the hospital with cancer. A Pentecostal minister, the woman lived near the hospital and came to pray with Julie. Together they waited for Mark to awaken from the darkness he had sunk into. When everyone else left, she and Julie kneeled by Mark's bedside asking the Lord in heaven to give Mark time to say his good byes. The time spread out and Julie wondered if Mark had passed beyond last words with loved ones.

"What are you doing here?" Mark, pale and barely visible between the white sheets was questioning her. Julie thought, I'm going to faint. *Oh, God send the nurse in before I scare him to death.* "I've been laying here in darkness," he said, his voice weak. Each word was a struggle. His eyes lifted to the line of clear tubes that hung from a fixture, following them down to his body, then straying to her face. "While someone fought the battle for me. Was it you?"

"Do you remember?" barely audible the question rushed past Julie's lips. She stood up, her legs unstable as she sank down by Mark's bedside. With her face near his, hot tears slid down her cheeks and mingled with his. And Julie remembered the days when they were children and clung to each other when the lightning struck and they were afraid. He was one and she could only have been six years old, all the comfort he needed then. "Tell me a story, Julie," he would say, "The one with all the golden promises." And she would tell him the story, first told to them by their grandmother and soon Mark's fretful breathing would even and he would sleep. But today? Where were the promises? Her mind cried out, at times unaware of the bargaining she was doing with God, other times sinking into a hopelessness she could neither explain nor dismiss.

"Julie, I've got to tell you something. I've been laying here, maybe unconscious, maybe it's the drugs. Somewhere, between here and there, I've made a decision." He swallowed hard, waiting for strength. "Years ago, I felt God wanted me to do something with my life. I wouldn't give it, Julie. I thought it was because of mine and Dad's conflict, but it wasn't." His hand searched for hers. "I wouldn't dedicate myself." His eyes sought Julie's for understanding. "Whatever time I have left, God can have it. Remember the promises, Julie? I made you tell the story over and over. The promises were always the same."

Mark went home. The doctors didn't understand how. They called it remission. Mark called it healing. Julie drove the fifty miles to sit with Mark up on the hill under his favorite tree. Lauren didn't mind. It gave her time to be with Brent. They were sitting under the tree watching the hay bailers arrive. Mark remembered the year before he helped the neighbors stack bales of hay on the trailer. "Higher than old Sam could pitch." Mark laughed. "You know Sam takes Brent swimming." He turned to her. "Julie, how do I look?"

She tousled his hair. "Well, you look good but how do you feel?"

"Good. Maybe I'm going to be around awhile, after all. I'm going back to work." His face became serious. "I called. They can use me. Lauren's the only one that knows. Then a twinkle dawned in his eyes, "I just need some help with the folks."

Julie groaned, "So that's where I fit in. Do you think that's wise?"

"I have to, Julie." Sweat stood on his upper lip, just like when he was a little boy. "Just tell them to lay off, will you, Julie?"

A flash back from their childhood, surfaced. Once when a sow had a litter; their dad had given them the runt. "Daddy says runt pigs don't live, Julie," Mark said bravely, "But we can love him until he dies." She had helped carry table scraps to the runt pig and fed it with a bottle and the runt pig had lived.

"There's something else," Julie said. "I almost hate to bring it up."

"What's wrong?" Alarm sounded in Mark's voice.

"We talked once about giving Mom and Dad an anniversary party on their fiftieth."

"Already?" He considered her nod. "Then let's do it. You plan it and I'll pay my part." He grinned. "After all, I will have a job, won't I, Julie?"

Planning the party was not the extra task she had wanted nor needed; instead it became an event that drew people together. The list that seemed long was divided into other people's lives smiling and pleased to be a part of the gathering. It was time to tell John and Sarah what was planned and who would be attending. Julie dreaded her father's outburst but he surprised her.

"So that's what James Haney meant when I saw him at the store the other day." John's eyes twinkled. "He said how about we play some of those old songs, John? I bet we can stir up some excitement." Her father lay his arm around her shoulder, peering into her face. "So you thought no one would tell?"

"What will I wear?" Sarah asked. "I don't have anything special."

"You have one week to figure it out," Julie grinned. "It's going to be very special. Your friends wouldn't let me and Mark go this alone. James and Harry have rented the Firemen's Ball Room. I didn't even know it existed." Taking a small pad from her purse, she ran the list. "On Mary Street, Dad?"

"Yes, it is daughter. That's where Harry and the group play on Friday nights." His eyes strayed to Sarah. "We haven't felt like going in a long while. Maybe it will help to see them. But that's a pretty large place, Julie."

"We need it. You have lots of friends."

The night of the party arrived and with it Harry's band. Marjorie Rice came with a five tiered wedding cake she placed beside Marie Coffey's sparkling punch in her own crystal bowl that stood on a pedestal a foot high off the table; surrounded by gold paper cups and matching plates. Ruby Hudgens placed throw away silver, it was gold of course, in a pattern around the back side of the punch bowl and thanks to Julie's table cloths and streamers hung previously, the Firemen's' Hall took on a festive atmosphere as the musicians warmed the instruments.

Mark was handsome in a tweed sport coat of mingled tan and brown, and the creases in the trousers he wore could have stood alone. With his hand on Brent, they watched as John and Sarah entered to the applause of neighbors and friends. Harry struck up a tune on the fiddle and the band played along.

"I will never forget this night," Julie whispered. "Mom and Dad are as in love after fifty years as when they were young. It shows." Julie sighed. "I am in awe of their grace as they waltz across the floor."

"More in love Julie," Mark replied and though he was smiling, Lauren on one side holding his hand and Brent on the other, she saw the sadness above the smile and Julie's heart ached.

"We have to take pictures," she said, ignoring his whispered reply to Lauren as their parents danced by,

"She's afraid I'm going to die." Mark tried to laugh but the truth was there might be no warning.

Chapter Nineteen

Mark going back to work gnawed at her conscience and she wondered what it was doing to her mother. Julie had pled his case as he'd asked her to; John Buchanan's mouth settled into a firm straight line. He went to the window to look out on the hillside. The hours, the strenuous work, why would Mark do this?

"Doesn't he want to live?" He didn't turn around, just stood there contemplating the months ahead. The doctors said there was nothing they could do, if Mark went into remission that's all it was, remission. He was aware of Julie standing beside him. Sometimes he thought he scared this one, too. Hadn't he tried, since Mark returned to keep his anger at bay? Clenching his teeth, going to the basement where he had a small wood working shop set up, to take his mind off whatever had set him on edge? But a man could only spend so much time in repentance, then, his spirit soared in denial.

John didn't understand where the quick temperament came from. His father was never around long enough to know if the trait was inherited from him, or was it as his mother said; why he didn't know how to be a father? Since Mark's surgery he'd prayed; his mind in a constant fury that his boy was going to die. It wasn't fair. Nothing in life was fair. *Ma, what would you say about this?* He could almost hear her, *one day when you least expect it you'll feel Mark's pain and then you'll understand your own.* But he didn't understand any of it.

Sarah came to the other side and as Julie was doing, the women put their arms around John's waist. He knew their hands would be entwined behind his back and tears were running down their cheeks. He didn't look, he knew. "Dad," Julie's voice came softly. "Mark wants you and Mom to let him do this. He doesn't know how long he will last at work but he feels he has to try. It may seem wrong to us but it's important to him."

Mark worked three months, losing weight, going once a week for the chemo that was destroying the good cells along with the bad. His hair fell out and he wore a three cornered handkerchief tied around his head, pumping up his arms to tease the children, "Hey, Mate, I'm a pirate going to sea." His arms were losing tone, the muscle gone. Lauren said the camaraderie of the men kept him going but when he couldn't keep up with the work load he worried he would be fired when the boss realized there were times the men covered for him, when he was doubled over in sick heaves. "Not a lot but sometimes."

Julie was on vacation, the day Mark drove down. Surprised when he entered, the words were out of her mouth before she could stop them, "Well, look at you. What are you doing here, middle of the week?"

"They laid me off." His shoulders drooped. "Lauren's at work. Brent's going to Mom's after school."

Hugging him, she led him into the kitchen. "Coffee?" He shook his head. "Tea?"

"I can't keep it down, Julie." He saw the sadness in her eyes as she closed the distance between them and hugged him. "Actually, the doctor told me it was time to quit. I was doing more harm than good to myself." He sighed, his body trembling as he hugged her tighter then released her. "I knew but I'm a man trying to prove my worth as symbolized by the dollar bill. How am I going to take care of my family?"

"Mom and I were afraid this day would come," her words came doused with tears that were unbidden but she had no control over them. She swiped a hand across her face. "What does the doctor say, at this point, Mark? He said he was in touch with the cancer experts, Oklahoma, Texas and one out on the East Coast, I forget the name."

"I'm dying, Julie. We all know that. The doctor thought I'd die on the operating table. Now he won't say how long I have, but I can't work. I talked to my boss. He said take as much time as I need but we both know I won't go back. I'm too weak." He clenched his eyes tight for a minute. "I'm too weak to hold a torch, Julie, to do the welding."

"Come on." She pulled him up from the chair. "We are taking a ride. We've been shut up in the work place too long. We have no idea the world has changed around us." She reached for her purse, pulling him through and shut the door behind them.

They rode in silence, no need to speak, their thoughts were the same.

Julie drove by the school they both attended, glancing his way as they smiled; seeing children at play. Back on the highway she headed toward the river where she had hauled grain for Blaine before taking the job with the newspaper. They met a car with teenagers in it, and one looked like Lissie. A quick intake and a small gasp brought Mark's attention to his sister. "Was that Lissie?"

"I wondered the same thing." The school is sending a few students to Central for special classes but I thought they were going over on the bus. That just won't do, what if they had an accident?"

"What's going on, Julie?" Mark saw the anger of the moment slip into sadness on Julie's face.

"You can tell?" She asked and he nodded. "We've reached a point, I don't know what to do, Mark. She's not exactly rebellious, but then again what would we call it? She doesn't like curfew, thinks she's old enough to make her own decisions and while she doesn't talk back, she continually goes against our wishes."

"Your wishes and Blaine's, or yours?" Mark sighed. "Remember how it was with me and Dad."

Julie's head jerked his direction. "I never mistreat her."

"You never would. I'm just saying the two of you are going through a trial and possibly Julie, Lissie doesn't know why either."

"What does Blaine say?"

She giggled. "He says she's the type, if we don't let her go and show trust in her, she will sneak out."

"Blaine said that? I'm surprised. Good old solid, stable and reliable Blaine?"

"I know. He says she's got too much of Myrtle Buchanan's independence in her and that she's a lot like me."

Mark laughed for the first time. "You never sneaked, did you?" He grinned as she shook her head. "Nah, we didn't have the chance, besides I got in enough trouble right out in the open and I never pulled the stunts Joe Lynn did. Bill and Letty suspected but I never told them about Joe Lynn's escapades."

"I've not asked, but you built a little heavy on Joe Lynn and the scripture thing. I know he loved to sing and that was his favorite song, but he never memorized scripture like you, Mark."

"He read it though; anyway let's say he heard it. Grandma took every opportunity when he was with me to take us aside and explain something. Joe Lynn listened to her where he didn't always his parents."

"Sometimes, even I thought he was too reckless but it seemed they couldn't curb his curiosity. That's why I worry over Lissie. I feel like I'm not getting through to her."

"Let me talk to her. She's a lot like me. I know you think she's independent but actually she's stewing and fretting while she thinks things over."

"Sometimes, I worry over her and I get so low in spirit I think there's no way out, then I remember Grandma saying, out of the shadows, into the sun."

"I would never have thought that of you, Julie, but it's happening to me more every day. I try to keep myself up for Lauren but she knows. We try to be so good to each other, then something happens and we act normal." He laughed. "I miss Grandma. If I didn't have you and Mom to keep me on an even keel," he laughed, "I don't know what would happen, but I will tell you this I've been talking to a lot of people about Jesus. It makes me feel better."

"Do you tell them you're sick?"

"If they haven't figured it out, why tell them?" Mark laughed. "You better take us home, Julie. School will be out and I know you are itching to check on Lissie. Right?"

They were riding along, when Julie chuckled. "I just remembered sassing Grandma and she slapped me. That was the only time and I deserved it. It wasn't a beat you up thing, just slapped my mouth."

"Do you think Grandma would be disappointed in me?"

"Never. Uh-uh. Not Grandma. To her, you were the salt of the earth. She loved you."

"She did, didn't she?" He sighed, contentedly. "Once in a lifetime that happens, ultimate satisfaction."

Poking him in the ribs, joy mingled with sadness, she said, "I think you're pretty special, myself."

"God knows I'm not."

"Why, Mark? Why would you say that?"

"You've done well, sis. But look at me." Mark laid his head back against the head rest, staring up at the ceiling of the car. "Dad found fault with me. For a short time, Lauren and I were so happy when I worked for the railroad out of St. Charles, then I'm sent to Korea, Cambodia and finally Vietnam."

"I always wanted to ask you about that, Mark, but you hear stories of how bad it was, so I didn't ask."

"I don't know why they sent us over there. For me, it was to watch a green hillside turn brown from chemicals. Strike after strike with millions of acres of land the people needed to make their living, burned. No one can imagine. They were a people caught between time and place with no future."

"Does it weigh you down?"

"I've tried to forget it. I didn't see what the guys in the Army did. I wonder what they remember. Once we were in the tent with the grunts in the other end and they'd heard stories. That was before the Army sent them into real conflict, boys my age; we gave up any bravado the uniform portrayed, we were just kids and those weren't chickens running for their lives in the backyard; they were real people."

"What hurt the most?"

"Having to leave my country, my family, and leaving Lauren. At least I came back." His eyes held hers. "Lauren and I had such plans. Since I've returned I've not even had a decent job. We have a government with the power to send its young men across the ocean to fight; you would think they could find them a job when they return?" Mark sighed. "It puts a bad taste in your mouth that they don't."

"You have a right to be bitter."

"Do I? I don't know. I wonder about it all and I ask am I weak in character that I've come full circle, still in the category I began when I graduated school. So many didn't come back and we that did are behind in everything, our marriage, our career and our lives."

"Grandma always had an answer. What would she say?"

A gentle smile lit his face. "I've asked that a million times and I hear her say, "One day with the Lord is as a thousand years and a thousand years as one day, we're all part of God's plan." He shook his head, "I don't know, Julie. Here, it's one thing, but over there I began to understand what she meant. Now I'm in the mainstream of life, a man with responsibilities, unable to do anything about them."

"Time stretches out," she said.

"It swallows us."

Blaine was sitting on the door step waiting for her that night. "Why the long face?" he asked.

"I've been thinking about things Mark said."

"He's turning." He sought for words of agreement. "He's almost too quiet. If I had a death sentence I would too."

"There are beans to put in the freezer and I can't seem to get my mind on what I need to do most."

"Julie, girl, as your grandma used to say, you need to take some time off from the Newspaper. Hand in a column once a week and let the job go for a while." He stared the direction of the garden. "Those beans out there don't matter. If you don't put one bag in the freezer, who cares? They are not your priority, this year."

She leaned into his side, thankful when his arm came around to draw her close. He had perspective when she allowed her own head to become all muddled. "I think I should be around for the folks."

"Those are my thoughts, too."

Taking Blaine's advice, Julie spent one day gathering material for a month of columns and handed them to the editor. "I hope you understand…"

"I wondered when you would decide you were needed, elsewhere. Keep us posted." His eyes were serious as he sighed heavily,

"Julie, keep notes, maybe a journal. Someday you are going to want to read what you went through with Mark's illness and knowing you it will have to be an accurate account."

In the week following, Julie finished the endless tasks she had let slide in the household. She was biding time, allowing Mark and Lauren privacy and her parents, too. Sunday church passed and Mark called on Monday. "Are you avoiding me, Sis?"

They laughed together. "No, I was waiting for you to call."

"Can you come up?" Wistfulness was in his voice. "I don't feel like driving today, Sis."

Her heart caught in her throat as she pushed down a sob. "I will be there by noon. I'll bring sandwiches."

"It doesn't matter, Julie. I can't keep food down."

Hanging up the phone, she pressed her head to the wall. *How can I do this? I love him and he's leaving. How can I go through this and be strong for him and Mom and Dad? Dear Lord, help me.*

Lissie entered the room, hair tousled from sleep. "Mom, do you care if I go with Jenny this afternoon?" Yawning she slipped into the chair to lean her elbows on the table. "Her Mom's taking us, if I can go, to look at formals."

"Formals? I had forgotten." Guilt's moment of pain made her stare at the floor. "Why now?"

"In case we have to order them."

"You know I'll have to check out the price." She saw Lissie's expression. "Agreed. Right?"

Lissie caught the bus to school and Julie left with a small cooler containing two sandwiches and drinks. Her mind shifted from the roadside scenery of aluminum grain bins, leaving farm land behind as she crossed the St. Francis River. Her parents had left the life they'd known together, over forty years, to learn the ways of the hills. More important than that, John Buchanan was seeking peace in retirement with his faithful wife and it was a blessing when Mark moved home for both of them to see him every day. Now every day would hold unrest and fear of losing their son, knowing it was going to happen.

Turning into the Burrows drive, she saw her father's truck parked down the lane by one of the fenced areas and beyond that the cattle on the hillside. He was probably mending a fence. She closed her eyes tight for a moment, praying subconsciously today would be good, no sudden change of atmosphere caused by her father's discontent or ill health that would lay heavy on all their nerves. Mom said he had no energy for temperament, John Buchanan had asked the Lord to spare his son and take him.

It wasn't peace flashed through her mind. It was remembering the day she had arrived to find her father livid over receiving papers from a loan company. Mark had borrowed money at a high rate of interest and unable to pay, the papers were sent to his parent's address. Her mother was crying, twisting the apron between nervous fingers. The memory was vivid. It would always be there.

"Stop your sniveling, Sarah." The fire in John's soul raged and burned bright in his eyes as Julie stood listening. "He shames us. Why can't he prove himself a man?"

"Didn't he do that, when he was willing to fight for his country?"

"You band against me, you, Mark and Julie. Does she know?"

"Daddy?" She'd listened enough. "Why are you saying such terrible things to Mom?"

"It's true, isn't it? You all tiptoe around, whispering, thinking I'm asleep, while you draw close to each other and leave me out."

"We never…."

He rounded the table. "Yes, you did. I could have helped him. I'm his father but no one told me."

"We didn't know." Julie stood her ground, not one to waver, as he neared. "If we had, maybe we could have kept him from leaving. Honest, Daddy, we did not know."

She shivered, remembering. John Buchanan had slumped into the chair and lay his head on the table and cried. "All I've ever done is hurt the boy. I wanted to love him but I always took things the wrong way." She could still see the trembling of his body, her mother standing with her hand on his back saying soothing words, trying to understand the wrath that claimed her husband while her heart broke for her son. And Julie, with her hand pressed to her lips until the knuckles turned white felt a sinking in her heart as she wondered, why? If he loved his son that much, why? And Lissie came to her mind.

Chapter Twenty

◆——————◆——————◆

"Hey, are you coming in?" Mark met her, grinning as his eyes lit up, but she saw the thinness and his skin turned a shade grayer than the last time. "I saw you staring towards the folk's house, anything wrong?"

"No, I think Dad's in the pasture. I was looking for him."

"I wish I could help him. Would you believe, he walks faster than me these days and him with cancer, too?" He hugged Julie. "Come on in, unless you want to sit under our old tree."

"Let's do that. I'll get the cooler." She saw him look away. "You don't have to eat Mark, but you might like a drink." Retrieving the cooler they walked to the old scrub pine. How many times had they sat here and he'd repeatedly told her before he left for service he and Lauren walked to the spot every day. She felt him stumble and saw his weakness as he finally sank down on one of the two rocks they had scavenged from the hillside, flat pieces of shale that fit solid to the ground.

"Julie, did I ever tell you what Dad said to me when he found me in Michigan?" *Mark didn't say when I ran away.* "He found me through the address on the letters where I sent money home to Lauren before she came to where I was." Mark paused looking out over the hillside. "It's all changing, Julie. Look. Last year we sit here through Sam's hay baling, the year before I helped him, now I'm so weak I can hardly get to this tree and I can't help Sam or Dad."

She was quiet. How could their thoughts have gone back to that time when Mark left home? If it helped him to go back and try to make sense of it, she could listen. Today he was wearing overalls. His stomach swelled and he couldn't stand the band that trousers made around his waist. "I have three pair of these," he laughed and explained. "Lauren keeps them washed up." His hair was trying to come back in and it was curly. But the third round of chemo had left him retching and unable to keep down food, against all hope the doctor said the chemo was not working, what did Mark want to do? Mark quit the treatment. "It's futile," he said, on that day, resigned and accepting his fate.

"Dad said, come home, boy." I was prepared for the usual press of guilt I always felt when Dad lashed into me verbally. I just looked at him wondering why would I go home, back to what I'd run away from? And Dad wavered and stumbled and I caught him in my arms. He said, "I need you, boy. Your Momma needs you." And I wondered what for? "Come help me with the cattle, maybe you can get a job on the side to make ends meet and I'll back off. Your Momma is dying inside with the way things are."

"He was hanging onto me, Julie, like a dying man and he speaks of Mom's concerns? Lauren was ready to move back. We were living in a cramped apartment with a scrambled arrangement of furniture we found on the streets when people threw them out and what we could buy from second hand stores, but we were happy. It was a decision I couldn't have made, except Lauren wanted to come home."

"Why didn't you tell me that day, Mark? You were at the house and I knew something was wrong but I was trying not to press you."

"I couldn't spit it out, Julie. I was dressed to go into people's homes to sell them insurance which they needed, but premiums are hard to pay and first payments even harder. I'd grown so tired of hearing peoples reasoning and my own sale pitch, I came to your house to get away from it all. Remember, when I left I was going to see Bill and Letty and you said, Bill's in the field, Mark."

His thoughts returned to that day, "Bill's working, love, remember?" Julie said. "Go on down to the field if you want to see him and Letty is probably home."

He had passed by, seeing Letty in the back yard. He'd experienced Mr. Ratliff's disapproval that morning. "I don't want your insurance," he'd snapped. "Can't afford it and you ought to be ashamed pushing something folks can't pay for. Get a real job."

It wasn't blood rushing through his veins; it was pain that seared his soul. Why didn't anyone understand he'd tried to find an honorable job? No one was hiring. Too bad he'd had a good job before he left for service, times changed, maybe it was due to the war and they'd looked at him like he was responsible for that, too. He had to go home. But no one was there. He couldn't go to his parents. He went to Julie's but he couldn't tell her about the rejections, the premiums unpaid which meant his salary would not cover their living expense.

He glanced at the brief case lying in the seat. In the back was a change of clothes, besides the suit he was supposed to drop off at the cleaners. Through the night he'd watched the hands of the clock creep slowly around, the morning would come and it was time he made a decision. The loan payment was due. In the moonlight, Lauren had turned her back to him, her skin glowing softly. He could reach out and touch her but she was worried too. Stress put a barrier between them. He knew she was awake, unable to sleep but there was nothing more to say.

There were no secrets. First had come the time of reasoning, how to work their way through the dilemma; then the blame until they were in an argument and stiff pride reared its head, word after word, blame and denial and last; the sharp silence. They had known rage and contempt but no tenderness. She arose for work the next morning leaving him where he'd finally dropped into nameless sleep worn out from the emotions they'd spent, sorrow in his soul, with no solution and no way out.

He folded the denim pants, the shirt, underwear and socks, a change of clothes if needed. He would speak with his father; face the consequences of rage over a loan company's charges. He would go to the office, pick up his mail, and drive by Lauren's office to see if they could catch lunch, a sandwich. He should never have driven by her place of work but he did. Now he was telling Julie what happened.

Parking out front, he turned off the ignition, wondering should he go in or leave matters alone. Self-persecution claimed him. Things were coming between him and his family. He filled out application for better jobs and as much as he tried nothing was coming from it. Joe Lynn flit through his thoughts. Joe Lynn had loved life in spite of a marriage that didn't fit. Now he was gone.

Lauren was hurting as much as he was, otherwise she'd not said the things she had, nor done. God in Heaven, there was no return. Then he saw her come out the door with a man and she was smiling.

"Why is it, sis, we talk the small things to death and the big issues we leave alone?" They were sitting under the pine remembering things better left unsaid. "We each suffered in silence, through my leaving, finding a job, writing Lauren through Sam." Mark laughed. "Sam could hardly stand the intrigue, trying to hand over the letters unnoticed to Lauren, while fearing Dad would be angry with him if he found out."

"Who was the man, Mark?"

"She does work for Moses Real Estate." Mark shook his head as he shifted his body on the rock trying to find a comfortable sitting. "The buyer returned to find his rep had gone to another town to show a piece of property and he asked Moses if someone else could take him out to the land?"

"You should have known if anything was wrong, a couple wouldn't meet at the place of business, would they?"

"Stranger things have happened, Julie. It took our lives straightening out, before we could discuss the issue. Lauren called it my lack of trust and I called it wrong. Now I understand I was insecure."

"Do you feel insecure now?"

"I don't know what I feel, Julie. I don't know how much time I have. I can't work. Lauren has to and that takes away from our time together." He sighed, staring out across the field of Mr. Burrows that joined his father's land. "On the good days, I get in the old rattle trap and head off on a back road and if I see someone walking, maybe mending a fence, whatever, I talk to them because it doesn't matter who they are I have learned to let the Holy Spirit lead me. If there's a receptive soul and the Holy Spirit sends the message through my thick head I stop and talk with them, ask if they know Jesus? We talk awhile and I go on my way." For a few minutes they sat silent while Mark reviewed the people he had met.

"There are a lot of back roads in these hills?"

"You wouldn't believe how many." He raised his head to meet her gaze. "Good people. Some seem almost backwards and then I find out they have sons and daughters they have sent to college, now with a degree and working in good jobs." He sighed. "But usually in a city where there's opportunity."

"What can I do, Mark, to ease your pain?"

"When I know you can drive up it helps." He lay back on the ground. "On the one hand I don't have much time to live and on the other, too much time alone. A person thinks and thinks and I wonder what was in my power to have prevented this disease and what was in my person to have prevented the problem all those years between me and dad?"

"Do you remember any good times?"

He rose up on one elbow. "There were. I do remember Dad picking me up and carrying me around. I must have been what, three? When we went to the family reunion and he was proud to show me off."

"The reunion happened every year, Mark and I was busy playing with the cousins."

"I saw a picture of you and Daniel." Mark laughed. "You were dirty, Julie, and Daniel was clean. I asked Mom what happened and she said the two of you had gone off alone and being curious when you found the grape vines hanging from the trees, the two of you tried to play Tarzan."

"My vine broke and I tumbled down the hill side. I remember. It's a wonder I didn't roll off the cliff."

"How old were you?"

"First or second year of school." Julie grinned. "I made Daniel promise not to tell. That worked really well when Mom saw my dress. It's a good thing they didn't send you with us."

"That is probably during the days I was dad's pride and joy."

"You're pretty droll about that, but I remember dad sitting rocking you, anyway with you on his knee while he listened to the radio; after his day ended and baths were finished we would sit in the living room and listen to the strangest programs. One was named Gilder Sleeves."

"See, Julie? We had normal family times. It was when the times got tense we thought they would never end. Tell me what happened when I left that day."

"It was the next day I got out of my car to walk up to the house and I heard Dad's voice. We always knew when his voice raised a decibel that trouble lay ahead; so I stopped and listened." She sighed, heavily. "I can still feel the quickening I felt in my heart that day, Mark. But it was the time in between that day and you coming home that nearly killed us. We didn't know if you were safe. We hoped surely you were well. But we had no idea where you were."

"Lauren was miserable. She continued to work. Mom kept Brent and Dad hired a private detective that evidently wasn't very good at his job because he didn't find you. You didn't leave any trail."

"I wanted to prove myself. You know, find an excellent job, make millions and everyone back home would feel they'd judged me wrong and my life would improve just knowing that." Giving a slight chuckle, Mark continued. "You know that didn't happen but I did have reasonable employment and sent money home to Lauren and that's how Dad found the address and the rest is history. Dad drove all that way to ask me to come home and I'm glad he did."

"While you were gone, Mark, Dad became silent, I guess best describes it. It was as if he was thinking things over once he had that initial outburst. I was surprised. Here was our dad who would move Heaven and earth to get what he wanted if it was within his grasp and he was quiet?"

"I was too, Julie. Sometimes you can't turn off the thoughts. They keep you awake, make you tired and go on night and day. I had to work to send home money and I was exhausted from thinking."

A scowl darkened her expression as she remembered; the community had its say. Unless Lauren's family talked they knew nothing but drew their own assumption. Gradually, Julie had become aloof, attending only the morning service at church with her family. And then one day, she felt a lightning of her spirit. Grandma's words came, *out of the shadows into the sun, girl.*

Laughter bubbled up, while Mark stared at her, amused. "What?"

"Grandma was talking in my head again, but I was actually remembering the day I knew everything was going to be all right. I called Mom. We talked a minute and I asked her how was Dad and she said he's sitting in front of the fire with a scowl on his face probably lost in thought."

"I said, Mom, let me talk to him. She must have handed the phone right over. "Dad?" I heard him move. "Everything's going to be all right. Mark's coming home." Dad actually laughed. Then Mom told me, Dad hired a second detective that located you but Dad wasn't sure you'd come home on your own, so our father was planning a little trip." Julie beamed. "Grandma was a little late on that one but it all turned out good that day. And you know what, Mark? Our mother said she communicated with you every day and she wanted to ask you if you felt her reaching out. Did you feel Mom's love?"

"She hasn't asked but Julie I felt Mom's love every day of my life. I'll take that love with me to Heaven." The smile on his face ebbed into a sadness in his eyes. "Do you think we will miss those we love in Heaven, Julie?" He drew a deep breath that wavered and trembled as it came out. "We know so little about it." Tears welled up in his eyes. "I know I have to leave all of you behind and I know one day you will arrive there, hopefully one by one because this family has had enough catastrophes. I miss you already, Julie." He swallowed hard. "And I always miss Mom, I love her. She would give her life for us."

"Maybe you won't realize we are missing, Mark. The Bible says there will be no tears in Heaven, we won't know sadness, and it clearly states time is different, so if a year is as a day in Heaven…that helps."

Mark grinned, "Does the Bible say no tears in Heaven, or is it the song? Think about it."

"You just be watching for me, brother and I'll look that up while we are waiting." Her eyes held to his face. "Please don't leave us, too soon, Markie. I love you and I can't imagine my life without you in it."

"What's worrying you sis? I kind of get the idea it's more than me."

"There's so much, Mark. Mom and Dad growing older. Lissie thinking she's grown. Sometimes it's more than I know how to handle." Tears spilled over and ran down her cheeks. "But losing you is the worst."

"What about Blaine? That part is good?" She nodded and he was relieved. "I really like that guy."

Somehow, Mark began to remind Julie of times from the past when they'd laughed and enjoyed life. "Laughter is good for the soul," she said, sputtering over a particularly embarrassing moment from the past. "I can't believe I can laugh about that now. Because I was humiliated."

"Little brother to the rescue," Mark quipped. "At least the cop didn't take you in for driving on the wrong side of the road." He grinned. "I didn't tell him you didn't know any better, that it was your first time out and you didn't even have driver's license." He lay back on the ground. "Yeah, I was a pretty good little brother." He turned his head to stare at her. "You know he really wasn't sure if you were on the wrong side of the road, because of the two drive ways. Maybe he thought you just did wide turns."

"It was the scripture you drew him into that did it. He forgot all about me. It's good he was a lay preacher."

The day ended on a good note. The remembering had not set Julie to crying, again, and Mark sustained his pride. No up-chucking lunch that day but he'd only eaten a fourth of a sandwich.

He called the next day. "Thanks, Sis. You take my mind off the terrible part of life."

Over and over, Julie listened to his voice on the machine. She had worked in the office at the Newspaper, gathering material for columns for the time when she would not be available. Shaking her head she wondered, exactly what was the worst part of his illness, but then knowing would be enough to sink most people into despair and her brother was driving back roads telling folks about Jesus.

The heat rose to high temperatures, and the visits were confined to the air conditioned house. It was just as well. Mark looked out onto the hillside; a summer storm had caused a limb to break off the Pine. "I worry about losing that old Pine," Mark said. "I have a feeling we are going down fast."

July fourth arrived. The family, Bill and Letty, joined with Lauren's family at their home. The men carried Mark on a cot to the shade side of the house. The weakness of his body was escalating. "I want to participate, for Brent's sake," he explained. "Don't worry about my strength. We can do nothing about it."

Finished with sitting the food dishes, she had brought, on the table; Julie went to sit by his bed. He had a red three cornered handkerchief on his head and wore loose khaki pants and a white T shirt. "Looking good, Amigo," she whistled, placing a kiss on his cheek. "What can I do for you?"

It was then she saw the tears on those dusky lashes. "Time, Julie, more time. I feel myself slipping away and I want to hold on for Lauren and Brent but I can hardly get from the chair to the bed this week."

What to say crossed her mind and nothing came that seemed right. She laid her hand on the sheet next to his fingertips. Mark took her hand in his. "I don't know what to do, Julie. Help me."

Chapter Twenty-One

Wherever she went, whatever she was doing, Julie's heart ached; unable to help her brother, the pain increasing, the side effects of the pills disturbing, there was no end to the problems he faced each day. The hospital bed arrived. Brent climbed up to be with his daddy. Hand on Mark's chest; he lay in the crook of his father's arms, patting gently. Lauren worked as long as she could. The family worried she was stretching herself thin and tried to help to lessen the work load.

Now the people came to his bedside, embarrassed to be well when their neighbor was ill and being years younger it concerned them greatly. They talked of the weather, church, death and new babies; salvation was discussed in a new vein because the lack of it was blatantly clear to those hill folks; if you didn't have salvation, you desperately needed it; it was the guarantee that closed the deal on death.

"You got that right, Mark," neighbor Tomlinson agreed. "Either stand up and be declared you've repented of your sins and love the Lord or be eternally doomed. That's what you said to me that day. I'm forever grateful." He twisted the old straw hat in his hands while tears ran down his face. "I suppose the rest of the world ignored me because I'm gruff and stand offish, but you marched right in there and told me how it is."

"Mark," Sister Joy Carol from the Pentecostal church had come to see him one more time. "I remember what you said; that in Jesus eyes I'm forgiven, in his heart he has taken me in. My sin will be forgotten and one day I'll live forever in his Kingdom." Tears ran down her cheeks as she bent to kiss his hand, the hand she had accepted that day as a lifeline when she was considering taking her own life and he had happened to drop by to visit her family. With mother watching she had followed Mark to the car and ask him had he ever felt so worthless he wanted to end his life? The tears running down his cheeks were the only admission she needed. He prayed for her as they knelt there by the side of that worn out old station wagon; on their knees beseeching the only one who could truly know their sorrows and she vowed she would live on and give the dark thoughts to the Lord. Mark said her sins were forgotten and good years lay ahead. It was God's promise.

Jacob and Mae Lynn lived around the hill at the knob. Folks called it that since it was the foot stool to elevated hills they called mountains; covered with tall pines and mostly uninhibited Mark traveled the roads wondering where each one led or taking a path he had not traveled to see what he might find. He found Mae Lynn sitting in the car with the new baby, while her husband walked a mile ahead to find gas. "You live around here?"

"Yes, sir, we do, she replied. "But our car kept acting up, Ralph thinks the gas hand is off kilter but he should be nearly here."

"I'll go on ahead and give him a ride." Mark found him, carrying a can full of gas, worrying his way back to the wife and new baby. "Starting a family is a huge responsibility. Do you attend church anywhere?"

"No, sir."

"Wouldn't it be a good time to start?"

"Yes, sir. How do we do that?"

"It's easy. Just take the new baby and go, people will take you in."

"We'd like that. Is that all?"

"There's the matter of Jesus coming into your heart. Do you know him?" Ralph shook his head, negatively. "Then I will tell you who he is."

The Hill people drizzled through Mark's dwindling life, some days one and other days several. It seemed they had been drawn to this thin smiling stranger who drove the back roads telling them about Jesus or encouraging them to return to church. "Jesus loves you." He'd say as he was leaving, that smile larger than the face that held it.

"We could tell he was sick," they'd say. "But he was friendly and he wanted us to know the Lord."

The air conditioner hummed and ran endless hours. July had come in with a bang beneficial of the celebration of the states but for Mark the heat only added to his discomfort. Brent sat snuggled by his dad while Mark dozed when the medicine was first administered to move restlessly in the chair when it waned.

As if by miracle, Julie was there the day a shiny black Jaguar drove up, a black man got out and started toward the door. "Mark. are you expecting anyone in a really nice car?"

"No," he laughed, "Most of my friends drive trucks, mostly old, some new."

Julie went to the door. The smile flashed as recognition dawned in the man's eyes. "Julie?" His smile broadened and she reached out both arms to pull him into the house. Putting one finger to her lips she pointed him toward the front bedroom where Mark lay staring out the window.

"Mark, let's see if you remember this guy? It did take me a minute but when he smiled, I knew."

The two stared at each other, necks bent, face forward; it was the best gift of the day.

"Frank?" Mark moved to try to get out of bed. "My goodness I thought you had fallen off the face of the earth. It has been years…" Frank was hovering over Mark, lifting him up off the bed. "My goodness, goodness," Mark's face was wreathed in smile. "Man. How did you get so big?"

"I tell my kids," Frank's voice still wore that pearl of Southern culture, "I grew because Momma fed me too many buttermilk biscuits growing up." Concern wrinkled his brow. "Did I hurt you? I was so glad to see you I forgot my manners and gave you that old bear hug we used to do. Don't guess you are up to wrestling, though, are you?"

"I'm all right, Frank. Sit awhile or right here, if you want," Mark pat the side of the bed. "I don't want to miss a single word you have to say. Julie says you are driving a nice car. What is it?"

"A Jaguar," Frank said, modestly. "And I paid for it, too, in case that's your next question."

"What in the world do you do to afford a car that pricey?"

"Well, I didn't rob a bank. I kind of fell into it when I met my wife whose Daddy is from France and came over here to start up a business." Frank's smile turned mischievous. "Now, you got to believe me, I work, but Janine's Poppa, work wasn't for him, so he said we had to learn the business, Janine and I."

"I'm proud for you. That's just great. Wish I could have met your wife, too."

"Not only is she watching the store, Janine is pregnant with our third child and the doctor didn't want her taking the ride. She's due next month and he wants no complications."

The hour seemed to pass too soon but when Frank saw the fatigue settling into Mark's body, and became aware Mark was beginning to stumble over his words, he stood ready to leave.

"Well, Mark, Chicago is a long drive. I'm going to get going. It has brought peace to my soul seeing you."

"Wish I could get out of this bed and hug you, Frank. Thank you for coming."

"I'll hug you, buddy." Frank fell on his knees by the bed. "Lord God help us." He embraced his friend.

Julie saw Frank out the door, aware of the tears in his eyes and his inability to voice the emotions.

She returned to the bedroom. "Why did you leave us?" Mark could barely get the words out, the pain was hitting fast.

"I thought the two of you had a lot to say after all the years of absence." She handed him two pills, and wondered if they would curb the excitement he had known seeing his old friend. His hand trembled as he reached for the medicine. She fell into the family's habit of acting as though they saw nothing, while her heart ached and she wanted to throw herself onto the bed beside him and wail.

"Frank said he would've been here earlier but he hadn't known until he ran into someone from our school and they told him I was sick." Mark shook his head. "Julie, it bothered him so much when I told him I have cancer there were times he could hardly talk. Then he realized it was taking my breath if I kept talking and he told me to hush that he would tell me about the years between us; which he did." Mark sighed as if the thought were unbearable. "He's had a good life and says Janine is the best thing God ever gave him, except maybe our friendship." Pulling the covers up to his chin, Mark yawned.

"You are tired." Julie sat on the edge of the bed, one hand on his as Mark reached up to thread their fingers together. "I'll ease on out of here as soon as Lauren comes home." Within twenty minutes she saw the medicine taking effect, leaning over she kissed his forehead. "You are the best brother ever."

"I love you, Sis," His words were almost too faint to hear. The visit had worn him out. "I'm going to miss you." Julie bent close to hear but Mark was asleep. Exhaustion had run its course but the medicine only last a short while, the more exertion the quicker the need, the less talk hopefully it last longer.

As he slipped into medicated sleep, for the first time she accepted the fact she had to give him up. She wanted him to live but not like this.

Julie drove the miles, tears running down her cheeks. She couldn't face her parents. In her best effort she called to tell them she would be down the next trip but today she needed to hurry home.

"Oh, Julie," Mom's voice sounded disappointment. "Just for a minute." With a feeble attempt at laughter, she said, "Next time, Mom. Love you. Love Dad."

Heart ache laid the wounds bare. Mark and Lissie. Mark thirty years old. Lissie nearing driving age. Lissie trying to curb her rebellious nature in order to have more freedom. Lissie going against the grain of their family expectations. Lissie. Lissie. Julie wiped the tears from her face as she realized she was driving thirty miles an hour according to the speedometer in a sixty five mile zone.

The words Mark had spoken when he awakened from surgery spilled through her thoughts. "I always wondered if the Lord could use me. I know there was a calling I didn't accept when I was still a boy at home. I thought I didn't answer that call because of my and dad's problems. It seemed like I never did anything right. I struggled. I never talked back, I just couldn't communicate. How was I to accept God's call if I couldn't please dad? It wasn't his fault, Julie; it was just something happened between us."

He had remembered those times again, today. "Shhh, Mark, don't be troubled over that now. There are more important things to think about." How many times had Mark reviewed his surgery, the beginning of a miserable existence had it not been for his love for the Lord. "You beating this disease is our main concern," she'd said then. "We have to figure out what to do."

Those first days had been without counsel or doctor. But Mark worried over something else. "I don't want people to think I waited until the last days of my life, to give myself to the Lord, Julie, but if He can use me I intend to do what He says and go where He leads." Mark's voice whispered the miles away.

"Time is getting near, isn't it Lord?" Julie spoke to the Lord, driving down the road with her eyes wide open. "I know you are preparing me. He's the age your Son was Lord, when his ministry began. I know you feel our hurt. I know you understand. My prayers are selfish, but I don't want my brother to die. What about his little son, Lord? Doesn't he need his daddy? I'm not being hateful, Lord. I just need to understand. The doctor said it's all through his body. Why, Lord? Why?"

The days became a tangle of trips to the house, unexpected episodes at the hospital, until finally the call for an ambulance brought their worst fears. Mark could neither force down food, nor eliminate it. His intestines became so full he was vomiting and after each occurrence he felt better for a while until the need repeated itself. There was no balance of food to satisfy the strong drugs. Morphine was administered as a pump brought body fluids from his excessively swollen body.

He was blind now. His hands moved toward whoever stood by the bed; Lauren on one side, Sarah on the other. John lingered on the outer fringe so dire was his pain he often buckled at the sight of the tubes carrying waste from his son. Lauren had to find time to spend with Brent. When Brent came to visit, the equipment was swathed in white sheets so as to not frighten him. He sat as close to Mark as possible and Mark used every ounce of energy to pat his boy's leg or smooth his hand.

"Can you see me, Daddy? Your eyes are white."

"I will always see you, son."

"Are you going away, Daddy?"

"Yes, and one day you will come to see me."

"Can I go with you, Daddy?"

"Not for a while, Brent."

Brent lay down by his father, careful not to lay on a tube or his daddy's hands. "Hold me, Daddy."

It was as if no one else was there. Tears were stifled, sobs were denied. The boy needed his father. The father needed his son.

"Daddy? Who will read to me and who will teach me what I need to know?"

"Your Momma, son. We've already talked about it. When you need me, you go sit close to Momma."

"I don't know how to miss you Daddy. I want to go with you and take Momma, too."

"I love you, son." Mark felt his heart breaking. "I always will."

"I love you, Daddy." Brent felt his daddy, gently rubbing his hand. Gently, gently and he fell asleep.

Mark dozed in and out of sleep the rest of the evening; the pain made him whimper until midnight his cries were heard down the hall. The nurses shut doors, the family was called. Sarah and John, Julie and Blaine had stayed with Lauren but the family had settled in a small visitors room down the hall to allow Lauren time alone with Mark. Brent was with Lauren's sister. When her parents arrived, Lauren stood by Mark's bed praying, Sarah sat at the foot of the bed. The pump had a sound of a clock ticking and Julie wondered had they all considered it's rhythm, the sound the loudest in the room those times Mark rest from the medicine. Was it the sound of life or death?

"Mom?" Mark sat up in bed, his blind eyes unseeing, as he waited for her voice.

"Yes, son?"

As though looking around the room, Mark called, "Dad?" John Buchanan arose from the chair nearest the door.

"I'm here, boy." Mark's gentle smile shone above the pain, the extreme gauntness of cheekbones, and the white of his skin.

"I'm going to be going soon." He looked up, toward Heaven as if no ceilings were there. "It's going to be good." The effort cost him and he sank back onto the bed.

Lauren pulled the cover over him as he fumbled trying to find her hand. "You know I've always loved you." Lauren nodded, tears streaming down her face.

"And I've loved you."

"I'm sorry, Lauren." It was a whisper but everyone in the room heard the whisper and the rattle in his throat.

It seemed like hours but by the clock the time was possibly twenty minutes. Mark became subdued. Everyone said good bye. The hand had become limp, the lips barely moved as the pump continued it's clicking sound and they knew he was slipping away.

"Hallelujah," he whispered, trying to rise as his head tilt upward. "They're coming. Hallelujah." From that moment on, a quiet hung over the room, the presence of death had come to rob the one they loved but beyond that, there hovered a stillness no one could explain.

Each person felt it as the wonder grew, that whoever Mark meant when he said *they were coming*, was good. Lauren's sobs combined with the drone of machines and the click of the pump. Death was near.

Julie remembered stumbling by Blaine's side as he led her from the room. Mark had taken his last breath at three a.m. in the morning hours. Exhausted and spent the family would go to their homes. Lauren's parents were staying with her and Brent. John and Sarah encouraged Julie and Blaine not to worry; they would be fine. Everyone should go home and try to rest.

"But they won't be fine," Julie mumbled. "There's a hole in our hearts, we won't be fine for a long time." She sighed, the tiredness was sinking in. "Blaine, can you tell Lissie?" She felt him nod. "Thanks." Her body was so tired she could no longer function. "I don't know how Mom and Dad are handling this." Drifting into a sleep where spiders spun webs, iridescent, the colors of rainbows, she saw her parents standing at the window staring out. Her words came slowly produced, reluctant and rebellious and she marveled in her weary state of mind whether her parents saw their handiwork.

Waking, she remembered the dream and questioned the meaning of the spiders...but Mark was the result of Sarah and John Buchannan's love and she could not feature a more wonderful person, kind and considerate...her brother was finally reaping the reward Grandma had promise; all the golden promises. How could she live without seeing him? She heard the quiet voice of her inner being say, trust me, Julie. Let not your heart be troubled. You believe in God, believe also in me...in my house are many mansions...

Today, Julie decided, she would come to grips with the loss of her brother. The hole in her heart would leave behind the sadness of death, the hope and faith she had claimed years ago must rise to defeat the darkness of her grief. Her family, her parents did not know the depth of her despair. Mark deserved better. He would expect her to rally and she would but getting there might kill her inside.

The scar of fresh dirt should be turning green over Mark's grave. The funeral had been a marring of everything she felt inside, an unrest that tore at her being; slapped at all she believed. Why, her heart cried out? Why did he have to die? She stood at the head of Mark's casket, leaving Lauren a wife's right to meet her husband's friends, neighbors and school mates. From ten o'clock in the morning until noon, she stood in that spot, shaking hands and accepting hugs and saying all the right things. But it wasn't until Lauren showed her the Bible that had belonged to her grandmother, Julie's mind settled down to the knowledge God intended for her.

"You need to read the letter we found in it, Julie. Maybe your mother knew but you will see why she hasn't told us." Lauren handed her the Bible and pointed toward a small room away from the people. "I think Mark must have read this when he came home and then had your mother store it."

Julie recognized the shaky hand writing of her grandmother.

Dear Mark, If you are reading this, it means I have gone on before you return from the war torn land they sent you to. I think of you often and my heart aches to see you. We miss you, grandson. I think maybe your daddy misses you most. It is as if his heart wanted to stop beating and his will to live ended the day you left but he will find as I did many times, it is God who decides when our time ends, not ourselves. Whatever happens in the days until I see you again; and I will see you again in Heaven where the streets are wide and people are happy and there are no sick bodies, until that day I want you to know how proud I've always been of you. The scripture you learned always blessed me to hear you quoting verses because in your eyes I saw your understanding and love for God, in your voice there was a reverence placed there I believe by God himself. I never loved you more than your sister but perhaps in a different way because our hearts yearned for the love only God can put in hearts that are troubled and seen years of sad encounters. Many things happen we don't understand, son, but God will wipe away our tears and put a peace inside of us. When we see him those things won't matter anymore. We have a loving family, Mark, they just don't know they are, sometimes, and I'm speaking of your Daddy. My pain has increased until I cannot sleep lying down of the night and I don't tell the family to allow their worry; they will know soon enough. All I've told your Momma is to keep my Bible, and not to open it until you come home to open it and should you not return my Bible is to be put in your casket. I'm sorry I won't see you again until Heaven. If I could just hear you say my name one more time it would bring such comfort to me. I will see you in Heaven, Mark. I love you. Granma

Julie let the car roll to a gentle stop, turned off the ignition and glanced toward the hill where Mark was buried. He would have appreciated the old scrub pine on private property a short distance away. She walked to the gray monument with its strange epitaph. The sound of Mark's voice flooded her mind; words, hopes and fears Mark had shared, day after day, sometimes weeks apart during his illness.

His little boy voice, "Daddy said runt pigs don't live but we can love the little runt, can't we Julie?" And as a teenager, "I don't know why dad and I have problems, Julie. You're the best, Julie." Leaving to go into service, he said, "take care of everyone while I'm gone." Then he had hugged her, whispering, "Who's going to watch out for me over there, Julie?" She had to let it out of her system. The flood gates were opened today as she stared at Mark's grave. "I'm dying, sis. I know it and I can't do a thing about it."

"But you've been doing so well." He fell into her arms. "You pulled through chemo. Remember, we acted like we didn't know you lost your hair and then we wore those silly caps."

"I've tried, Julie. It's been so hard; in and out of the hospital, the chemo, worrying over everything, loving Lauren. We just hold each other and I want to hold everyone it hurts so much. I watch this old tree, Julie. I see it from our bedroom window. The winds sweep against it and sometimes I'm afraid it won't stand." Fragments of conversation battered and burst upon her.

"When I was little I begged you to tell me over and over all the golden promises. I think they meant Heaven. I don't know why I have to leave Lauren and Brent, but I've accepted God is taking me home."

She leaned across Mark's bed, kissing the taunt skin on his forehead. He searched for her fingers. She kissed his cheek. "I'll see you in the morning. I love you."

Mark's eyes were white. The blindness had claimed them as quickly as the cancer claimed his body. She heard him whisper the words. "I love you, sis."

She fell on her knees. What had he said? *"Don't you see, Julie. We have to talk about it." His voice was hoarse, the pleading in his eyes deep. "It's eating your heart out and mine too. You have to let go. We don't understand God's plan. I don't know why Brent won't have a daddy or why I'm leaving Lauren but my body can't last. Let me claim the promises, Julie. They are for you, too. Claim them and live. Don't mourn. The scripture says there's a time to every purpose. Other people need you, Julie. You have to be strong. Watch out for Lissie and Blaine. Love my little boy. Understand what Lauren has to do."* That was the last time they'd sit under the old scrub pine. Last week Mom said the pine fell. Dad had given up. She couldn't do that to Blaine and their children. A time to mourn must end. A time to live on was now. God had been patient with her. She would claim the promises but she would never forget her brother. God didn't expect her to and she would listen to His voice.

"Write about it, when you are ready," her editor said. "We all suffer through grief. We all need help."

Once more she read the epitaph imprinted on gray stone. *The poor man cried and the Lord delivered him from all his troubles and he received all the golden promises just as the Bible said.*

"I'm not here, sis. I'm with Jesus." She could hear Mark's laughter as she walked toward the car. *"One day you will wonder why you wasted so much energy missing me, Sis. I told you, God is in control."*

Julie turned the key in the ignition. Where had it all begun? Where didn't matter. For Julie and Mark it was on a farm, and Mark's hiding place where he memorized the scripture Grandma chose for him. "They that wait upon the Lord shall renew their strength; they shall mount up with wings as Eagles; they shall run, and not be weary; and they shall walk, and not faint. Isaiah 40:31

The End